The Glass Is Half Full And Frozen

By Edward DuCoin

THE GLASS IS
HALF FULL AND FROZEN

EDWARD DUCOIN

I started my first business as a college freshman, and with the help of a few truly great people - like my brother David, turned a few hundred dollar investment into a company with more than $20 million in annual revenues.

Although loosely reflecting my own life, this book is fiction. My goal is to offer practical information I have learned, sometimes the hard way, on how to become successful in business and in life. I wanted to do (this) in an entertaining way. So, within the confines of watching a struggling start-up business, you'll join Jacob Edwards, his family, Jacob's business team, and a man named Duke as they learn business, life, and relationship secrets. Hidden between the lines is a blend of theory, fact, and practical applications of lessons learned.

How did I do it? Well, while my friends studied the sports pages and *Playboy*, I studied Drucker and Peters. Okay…so I, too, played a bit. But I truly loved then, as I do today, the study and application of philosophies in team development and leadership skills.

As time went on, I not only wanted to study business and leadership concepts, but I wanted to *develop* them. Not long after this initial awakening, I designed a corporate training program to help bring my team members to a new level of performance. That training program became the foundation of a company that I took from corporate headquarters (a spare bedroom in my parents' house) in 1984 to a NASDAQ publicly-traded company in 1998. Many of the secrets in this book can be traced back to that original training program.

In 1998 my company joined forces with four other firms to go public in what is called a roll-up. Our investment bankers were Lehman Brothers and Montgomery Securities both top-shelf firms with great competence and contacts. Because of these contacts, I was able to befriend Howard Clark, Vice Chairman of Lehman. Mr. Clark sat on our Board of Directors and was a continuous voice of reason and common sense. For this reason, I made sure I sat next to Mr. Clark at every Board meeting. Not only did I want to contribute as a Board member, but I saw this as an opportunity to learn from someone who has been doing it right longer than I had been alive.

Most people fail to take advantage of opportunities to connect and learn from people with real-world, tried-and-true life experience. The mere fact that you are reading this book tells me that you are not one of them. As your reward, if you stick with me until the end, I will give you *tools* that far exceed anything you expected to get from a little book. Oh, there are many obvious tricks in the text such as "sit next to key people." But it's the *not-so-obvious* tricks and tips that I hope will positively impact your future.

You've probably heard the saying, "When a student is ready, the teacher will appear." I have a similar one that I want you to think about as you read this book: "When the mind is ready, the thoughts will appear." Now, you might already know some of what I am going to share with you, but I'm here to joggle your thinking and to get you into action. Thus, I can show you how to *apply* what you know. Let's unfreeze the ice in your half-full glass!

Why don't you be the judge? I dare you. Put these philosophies to an earnest test, and see if they will make a remarkable difference in the way you succeed. I hope you enjoy the story and your life is positively affected.

Edward DuCoin

Marlton, New Jersey

To Michele, thank you for your love, laughter, and commitment.

To Emily and Edward, nothing matters to me unless it is leading to your health, joy, and development.

To David, my first business partner, any value I bring to this world is based on the foundation of your character.

To my family and friends, I would trust each of you with my children, which is the highest compliment I can offer.

To my clients, your trust is the fuel that feeds the fire of my commitment to your achievement.

To my team (employees), your passion, trust, commitment, and spirit both energizes and humbles me.

THE GLASS IS
HALF FULL AND FROZEN

CHAPTER ONE

Friday, September 9

Checking Account Balance: $580,123

I love that Philadelphia is my home. I love the history, the food, and I love the sports teams. But I love this town most when I consider Philly is a town of second and third chances on the way to success. We're the Rocky story. We're the town of dozens of drafts of the Declaration of Independence. Near Philly, the Revolutionary War looked bleak and then turned to victory. It's a town where failure is embraced for the promise of eventual success. In many ways, Philadelphia represents the prototype of the American dream.

Before my business life began to falter, back when I was featured in *Success Magazine*, I'd walk Independence Park think about my unlimited potential. Soon, I walked the park only trusting in the mantra of perseverance because my life never looked bleaker. Although I had two beautiful kids and a wonderful wife, my business dream seemed to crumble with every step I took.

On the day I was to make a speech at the Wharton School of Business, in front of hundreds of MBA students eager to hear how a Wharton grad had made it big, a small article ran in the back of the *Philadelphia Business Journal* questioning the stability of my business. The writers of that article picked up on things I'd denied for months. My prayer was that none of these students had seen the small clip. My worst fear was that in the weeks to come, the doubts raised in the article would prove true. People love to watch a falling star. As a part-time race car driver, I knew many fans loved the thrill of fiery, smoke-filled accidents, metal crashing against metal. Business failure is observed in much the same way.

Earlier that same morning, Louise Aldridge, my assistant, walked in after I'd read the article.

"Jacob, you see a ghost?"

"I wish. I could use one of those Dickens' ghosts about now: past, present, future and all that."

She sat across from me, putting off whatever she was going to say. "What's up, boss? I've only seen this look a couple times the past ten years."

"I can't seem to get this company off the ground. Between us, I wonder if I've run out of luck. I can't seem to interest one single venture capitalist in this gig. Only a few have taken second looks, and even those are shaky."

"Think about it. In the first company, you had moments like this didn't you? Moments before the millions?"

I had thought about it. Hard. I could only remember the money seemingly flowing from everything I touched. I'd wake up, work twelve hours, and money was everywhere. Instead of analysts questioning my future, they would write phrases such as 'the boy wonder,' 'one of the country's most successful young entrepreneurs,' and 'dynamic with absolute determination.'

"I don't remember moments like this." And Louise didn't know half of how bad it was. But everyone on the team would soon find out.

She said, "Let's turn your biggest fears into opportunities. I need you in top form. We all do."

"My biggest fear? Look out the window. The last couple days I've noticed this older man doing nothing, just sitting and feeding the pigeons. There. The man with the purple hat. See him? It seems as if he keeps looking up here at me. Like he's staring into my window. My biggest fear is that I end up down there someday."

"What? Afraid of spending nice afternoons sitting around feeding pigeons? I can think of worse ways to retire."

"I'm just afraid I'll be there before I'm ready. Like in two months."

"If your biggest fear is ending up homeless in two months then you need to get over that. Because if you're homeless then I'm homeless. And we won't allow that. You're over-thinking right now, Jake. You could use a little kicking back in the park feeding pigeons."

I arrived at my speaking engagement late, but in time to ease everyone's mind that I was there. I read their eyes, watching for doubt, hoping they hadn't read the article. Nobody had, it seemed, or they politely avoided the topic. The Dean of the School introduced me as I stood behind the curtain feeling like a phony.

"It's always a pleasure introducing a successful graduate. Our guest today certainly falls into that category. He has been featured in *Success Magazine* and *Inc. Magazine* and has earned numerous personal and corporate awards, including being named as one of the most successful entrepreneurs in New Jersey and Pennsylvania under the age of 40. His most recent accomplishment was an induction into the Philadelphia Business Hall of Fame."

My stomach flipped, and I thought I might get sick. This had never happened. A businessperson should be able to adapt to change, and I always had. I couldn't shake the feeling though that I'd brought the current struggles on myself. I could have avoided them, somehow, if I'd personally done something different. Mistakes caused by others can be more easily seen and fixed. But if we fall into destructive habits, we often can't see our own mistakes. Had I taken up these same destructive habits leading to my failure?

"He started his first company as a freshman right here at Wharton with just a few hundred dollars. He eventually turned that into a multi-million dollar organization that went public on NASDAQ. The following year, he sold the company and pursued his dream of starting and racing with a NASCAR team. Now, along with the NASCAR team, he has returned to his entrepreneurial roots and started a new company based here in Philadelphia. Here to tell us the secret of his success, would you please welcome to our stage, Mr. Jacob Edwards."

And at that moment what brought me to this point kicked in- that God-given confidence. I spoke from rehearsed places, and their ears took it all in. They were captivated, enthralled, and inspired. I nailed it. As they stood with a hearty ovation following the speech, I was confused. Where did that confidence and those words come from? I was on autopilot on the stage.

What I wanted to say as an epilogue was that at this very moment I was losing thousands of dollars a week and had zero customers. I was more in debt than anyone in this room, and the German sports car I drove that read "Alumni of Wharton Business College" might soon be for sale cheap to the next *Wunderkind* because, boys and girls, I fear my luck has run out.

Before walking the steps back to the office, I sat across from Independence Hall upon the same bench on which the man in the purple hat usually sat. Men in suits crossed quickly in front of a horse-drawn carriage.

I didn't often sit at this time of the day. My normal routine consisted of team meetings, calls, speeches, proposal writing, quick updates from my accountant and, if time, lunch with my team. After work I'd head home to help my son Jake with homework, toss around a basketball with my daughter Emma, and respond to emails and letters after all had gone to bed, or until my wife Shelly said it was time to stop working. I always balanced time with my family and time at work. Suddenly, I'd found myself struggling to find quality family time.

When a pigeon landed near my foot, followed by second and then a third, I jumped to my feet. For a moment I saw my future. The only thing I lacked was a handful of crumbs.

I cut across the lawn in front of Independence Hall calling Louise on my cell.

"Got a favor, Louise. Pull the team together for a quick meeting in the conference room."

"Speech went well?"

"I wowed 'em."

"Nice!"

I had no idea what to say when I walked in, but everything within me said that moment on the bench was too symbolic of where the business was at that moment. We had to move forward.

Had my previous successes all just been luck? That would certainly explain the recent change of events. Maybe I had hit on something by luck the first time out and didn't know how to find that magic button again. I could make afternoon calls to some professors that attended the speech. And there was David. Even though these days he only tells me the books are heading in the wrong direction, he's worked as my accountant through it all. I needed guidance, and I didn't know where to go.

The inside of the board room was our most lavish display of affluence. The team walked in, and sat in large leather chairs with no idea we could no longer afford them. The elegant chairs surrounded a heavy, richly-grained conference table that spread across the entire length of the room. Hardwood paneling framed expensive artwork highlighted by track lighting. Sitting in the opulent environment, the crew chatted, but in low tones. They didn't know what I was going to say any more than I did.

"We've got donuts, hot coffee, fresh orange juice," Louise said handing me a cup of juice, "and some other goodies over there. Just like you like it."

"That was amazingly fast."

"I got it all lined up anyway for the venture capitalist meetings you're planning. Thought we'd set it up for your approval."

"I approve. Pass the donuts."

This room easily rivaled most of the better offices around town. "This is the finest looking team in all of Philly. You guys look primed." As I fell into the head chair I said, "Somebody give me an update."

Julie Barnes, new hire and HR Director, started. This was her first start-up, and her naïve innocence and ambition impressed me.

"I posted the public relations position on Monster.com. Keep your fingers crossed."

"Did you put it in the Philadelphia Inquirer, too?" Louise asked.

"No, I haven't." she answered calmly. "They're pretty expensive, so I thought we could try Monster and see how that works out before spending the extra money."

"I'd rather you just do them both right away," I said. "We need to get our public relations strategy in place. And while you're at it, be sure you list the Director of Sales position, too."

Everyone at the table shifted a bit.

After a couple of housecleaning questions, the tough questions started. I knew people were jumpy after the article this morning, but I was a little surprised by their forthrightness. Bob Fisher, our Chief

Technical Officer said, "I'll speak, Jake. We're a little concerned about a couple of issues. One is this hiring frenzy that doesn't seem to match our workload requirements. Maybe you could explain the strategy?"

"And while we're on the topic," Julie continued, "in my experience, limited I'll admit, most experienced sales directors don't go for pavement pounding cold-call jobs. All we have right now are cold calls."

"I don't see where we have much choice," I replied, studying facial expressions. "Right now we need someone who can lead. We have a new product and no formal sales protocol, commission structure, or training material. Without a leader, who's going to handle sales? I'd love to do it, but I'm buried up to my neck in fundraising issues with these venture capitalists."

Louise, always there to call me out, tilted her head a bit to the side as she asked, "So, if I understand you correctly, you're busy raising funds so we can pay someone else to do a job nobody can do as well as you can?"

I took a sip of juice as I pondered her comment. She was right.

"I never thought of it like that," I said. "But what else can I do? The Venture Fair is near, and I'll need to have someone here in time for the presentation. What should I say when they ask me about my sales team? I take a bow and say 'you're looking at him'?"

"Jake, I can't tell you what to do," Julie seemed to be measuring her words carefully. "I've never worked for a start-up before. It seems we're only interested in raising money. Do we need money that badly?"

"It took me and my brother twelve years to get my last company going well enough to make a decent living. This time I can't wait that long. *We* can't. Business doesn't work that way anymore."

My hotshot computer programmer, ambitious but cocky Otto Mason, spoke up. "With all respect Jake, you seem only concerned about raising money. You've missed two important management meetings. The team, and I speak for Bob specifically, could use your insight and experience in these meetings. We trust you, but since we're here and talking, we could use your CEO expertise."

The squirming around the table ended in motionless people staring at their notepads. Louise scribbled something. I hadn't expected much from this meeting certainly not an assault. This was new for me, and red flags waved all over. I couldn't risk this team walking.

"Bob, the rest of you, do you really think I'm that far off the mark?"

"Your goals, our goals," Bob answered, "are intact. There is no question we believe in you and this company. Personally, I believe in your sense of values, and I respect your business savvy. You know how to make things work. When you hired me you told me we were a team; We all work together, and we make it work because we watch out for each other.

And the other point you made…"

It was the same speech I gave all new employees. We were all part of a team, and the team was only as strong as its weakest link.

I braced and asked, "Are you suggesting I'm our current weakest link?"

"Tell you what," Louise said, "let's refocus on our individual projects for the purposes of this meeting."

"Thanks Louise," I said, "but we have this in the open, and we need to resolve it."

"Jake, I don't think you're a weak link," Bob said. "Without you this whole company would fall apart. You're the glue that holds us together. You're very concerned with our well-being, and you're doing all you can to make things work. I just think you're pushing as hard as you can in a direction that even you don't feel is the right one."

"Others?" I asked.

Otto said, "Did you know that Bob and the tech team worked all weekend to make sure you could test the demo before your presentation?"

I paused before answering, "No…I didn't know that."

Our Director of Marketing, the next busiest woman in the room, had remained silent. "Elaine," I said, "you never let me down. Tell me what's on your mind."

"Jake, I agree there's a lot going on around here that you're not aware of-things employees expect their CEO to notice. Bob and his team didn't come marching in here weekends asking for a medal. Every member of that team ran the extra mile because they believe in you and in this project."

"Really," Bob said, "we shouldn't focus on one specific area."

"No," I said, "we should. Because I dropped the ball, and I'm letting you guys down. We needed this talk. Somebody take us to our bottom line, and let's work upward."

"It looks to me," Elaine said, "like you're working your tail off trying to impress the venture capitalists."

"They have the money we need," I said.

"I'm looking for logic here. The economy suffered because of the dot com collapse. Most of those companies were backed by the same venture capitalists you're working around the clock to impress."

I paused. "Okay."

"Then why is it so important to get them on our side?" Elaine continued.

"Our entire business model is built around raising funds," I said. "Getting the package together is part of the process involved in giving favorable presentations. If we planned to grow slowly, I wouldn't need some of you."

They sensed my anger and frustration. I couldn't communicate that the anger was mostly with myself. I had no idea the complete business model was questioned organization-wide.

I'd been saying for years, from the moment I walked into my first shabby office, that the purpose for being in business was to obtain and retain customers. Without them, you aren't in business. And at this point, we had no customers. Furthermore, I had an unhealthy desire to impress venture capitalists and no other option for capital, because this is where I'd led us. I didn't want to restructure, but the headlines would grow bigger if I didn't do something.

"I need time to make some calls, gang. Thank you for your honesty and concerns. You must know that I value your opinions and creativity."

I left the room followed by silence.

THE GLASS IS
HALF FULL AND FROZEN

CHAPTER TWO

Monday, September 19

Checking Account Balance: $501,059

The man in the purple Phillies hat sat with his legs stretched, the warm autumn sun tanning his arms as he tossed soft pretzel crumbs to the gathered flock of pigeons. His face was practically covered with prescription sunglasses that made me think of flies. Buzzing fly-eyes on a human form, and if you slip his shirt off, wings would sprout, and he'd fly to the nearest dumpster. He sat, seemingly in his own thoughts as I stared from my window, wondering what that must be like to sit all afternoon in your own universe. I wouldn't know.

All the previous week I'd pondered that fateful meeting, and I'd come to a sobering conclusion. No matter what the team felt, up to this point we'd built a plan dependant upon raising funds, and I had to prepare for the upcoming Venture Fair. We'd reached the point of no return.

For years I've told people that it's not where you start, it's where you finish. That was my excuse for taking fourteen years to take my first company public. Not bad for a $102 investment. I always told people "less than five hundred dollars" because few believed the exact amount.

Fourteen years. Not acceptable to a start-up in our modern world. The modern definition of success is retired and living on an island or owning an NBA team before thirty. Yes, I had my NASCAR team, but I risked losing that as well. I risked losing everything in this climate where one was expected to move from concept to vast wealth within a few years. I burned my own cash on a daily basis. My portfolio was one-third its value of a year ago.

"Jake," Louise burst into the office. I removed my headphones and could barely hear. I must be the only CEO who knows every word of every Linkin Park song and who listens to music loud enough to disturb Dale Carnegie in his grave. Carnegie, the guy who said, "Develop success from failures."

"You can't hear the phone ringing off the hook?" she asked.

"Sorry. No." I held up the headphones.

"David's here. I offered him coffee and had him fix it himself while I found you."

"I don't know why you bother asking David if he wants coffee. He always wants coffee, and he wants it black. It doesn't even matter if it's hot or cold."

"Yeah, well, I wasn't sure what I'd find when I walked in here," she answered. "David was real impressed by the mugs with our logo on them." She didn't try to hide her sarcasm. "He wants to know our return on that investment."

At that moment, David pushed open the door and poked his head in.

"David, come on in." I opened the door all the way and shook his hand. "We were just heading out to meet you."

"It's okay," David interrupted, "I've been here a few minutes, just being nosey and looking around." He raised his other hand and ran his fingers through his full head of graying hair as he greeted me with that old familiar grin. "At my age, if you need a guide to get around, you're in a lot of trouble."

The warmth in his eyes dominated the room.

"How are you?"

"I'm fine, Jake." He looked over my office for the first time. "This is quite an office."

"I think we're all pleased, aren't we, Louise?"

Julie walked in, her smile also adding something to the room. She handed me a file report. The mood changed though, since I knew David was going to give me a lecture. I felt like the son who overspent on his first car, and David was the father watching me learn my lesson.

"You've met Julie, our Director of Human Resources, haven't you? This is Julie's first start-up, but she's hanging in there," I said as Julie shook David's hand and gave him a warm smile.

"It's great to finally meet you," she answered. "Jake talks about you like a father."

David smiled and answered, without missing a beat, "Well, I'm old enough to be his father."

"Let's go out and meet the rest of the clan, shall we?" I led the way as Julie, David, and Louise followed. I played tour guide as we made the rounds to each office. Then David and I headed to the conference hall.

"Well, that's us in a nutshell. An amazing team for our being in business nine months," I said, as I added a little flair to emphasize the opening of the door to the conference room. I tried to steal a glance at David's face to see if he looked impressed.

"We've got donuts, hot coffee, fresh orange juice, and some other goodies over there," I pointed, trying to sound as casual as possible.

David walked to the goodies' table and picked up one of the fine crystal glasses. He held it up to the light like a jeweler looking for flaws. "Jake, you shouldn't have gone to all this trouble. I'm fine with coffee in a Styrofoam cup."

He put the glass down and turned to look at me. The man who moments earlier controlled the room with his laughter, now stared at me with eyes that could penetrate the thickest deception.

"Is all of this to impress the venture capitalists, your customers, or me?"

David had always been able to see through me, and that's why I trusted him as if he were my brother.

"First impressions are everything. I'm sure you agree that if we're going to raise funds with venture capitalists, then we need to attract the right kind of people." I sat at the conference table, signaling for David to take a seat.

David answered, "So tell me, Jake. Are things really as good as they seem? How are sales coming along? Remember, I have some of the numbers, but you haven't sent me any revenue figures yet."

"We haven't made any sales. We're still in the start-up mode." I tried to make it sound as if it all fit neatly into some master plan.

David looked surprised.

"Are you kidding?" He lowered his voice and pressed his lips together. Once he surmised I wasn't kidding he said, "When I met you, you were eighteen. You bragged about how you had your first client within three days of starting your business, and how you had earned your first check within two weeks. You've been running this business nine months, and you haven't made a single cent? Why in the world not?"

"It's a different time, David," I said. "We're still in the product development phase. It has taken time to get the right team in place. I've developed a business plan and am currently trying to raise funds in order to move forward. It'll come together."

We had struggled and celebrated more than a few victories together. He had earned the right to be direct.

"Why are you spending time raising funds when you don't even know if you have a product the market needs or wants?"

"This is the new era." I looked at David hoping to sell my master plan. "If I don't attract investors, we're going to look like fools."

David pushed back in his chair, raising an eyebrow. "I guess we're going to have to see about this internet speed approach to business. I've been at this much longer than I care to admit, and my experience is that business comes and goes in cycles. I'm not sure I believe the internet is going to change that age-old rule."

I answered quickly, almost as if begging for a breath of fresh air, "I believe in cycles, too."

"Jake, let me be completely honest. I've been around Wall Street for a long time, and I suppose you can say I have seen it all. But what I'm looking at today puts me on edge." He stroked the leather arm of his chair. "These chairs are impressive, and those crystal glasses make a statement. But as your accountant, I have to ask where the money comes from for this show. You're a better businessman than this. There is a difference between a sustainable business and a traveling medicine show. One lasts; one is just spectacle. What's the rent on a place like this?"

"David, I hear what you're saying. But at some point, don't I earn these kinds of digs?"

I knew as I said it how foolish it sounded.

Before my eyes, in ten days, I'd watched my business make discouraging news, my team question our current direction, and my offices fade from my grasp. Even in my own eyes this looked phony, and I was scared it would show to investors. I felt like the Emperor in his new clothes.

"Jake, you have a nice house, nice cars. Hell, you even have a race car team. You earned everything you have. Now, the test is to not lose it." He leaned against a chair. "This leather is stiff. You could have at least bought soft leather."

"I get it."

"I'm sorry. I'm just surprised at all this. The first concept in accounting is that a business is its own entity. It's like another person. That's what's going on here, too. But you've got a child that hasn't earned a penny and yet is living like a spoiled rich kid because it has a funding angel."

"I have a great Board of Directors, a strong team, an impressive track record, a beautiful office, the best technology money can buy, and determination. But nobody wants to invest, and they're not interested in my experience or even in our business model."

"Then why are you continuing to fund the company? VCs are scared to death. You're looking for funds at the wrong time. Let me see a copy of your leadership training program. I liked the one you were using in your last business. What did you call it? *The Fluid Plan of Success?*"

"We haven't done a training program yet."

"That was your hallmark! That program helped develop your team and led to your success."

He sat back down and removed a folder from his briefcase. "I almost saved it until you were in better shape. But, I think it's time for a serious wake up call. Here are the financials. Right now you're spending $91,000 a month. If someone walked in that door today and offered to invest, the soonest you could expect a check would be at least 120 days. Four months. Add it up."

"I have a presentation with Michaels & Company two days before the Venture Fair. Bob and the crew put together a terrific presentation. Or, so I think. I haven't taken time to look at it yet."

"Even if you meet with them today, you're still going to be without funding until January."

David slid the financial reports to me. "I'm looking for solutions, Jake. And from where I'm sitting, there aren't many workable answers here."

"Can we grab a bite to eat? All of this has made me hungry." Trying to remain optimistic, I started to get up. "Besides, I promised I'd buy you lunch."

David chuckled, "Jake, you can't afford to buy me lunch. I recommend you get used to brown bagging your lunches for a while."

I put my hand on David's shoulder. "You are definitely right, but I'm gambling that if I buy you lunch, you might give me a break on your hourly rate."

"This one's on me for old time's sake." He walked to the coffee table as he continued, "I'll take a couple of these fancy Danishes with me, head on back to my office, and we'll call it even. Let me know how it goes with Michaels & Company."

"You know, you're right about the soft leather."

He turned to look at me. "How's that?" he asked with a puzzled look.

"Well, the way you and everybody else keep kicking me in the ass, the least I can do is make sure I have something comfortable to sit on."

David gave me one of his reassuring smiles as he turned to leave.

"Get to work."

THE GLASS IS
HALF FULL AND FROZEN

CHAPTER THREE

Monday, October 3 - evening

Checking Account Balance: $469,921

It was almost a month after my team alerted me to our major problems, when a shift took place. I was staring at the sun that seemed to be sitting atop the office building across the park, when Purple Hat looked up into my office window and waved at me to join him. Startled at first, I then decided to head out and chat. Louise said I could use some kicking back with the pigeons. Perhaps a break would soothe my curiosity and help delay my overtime efforts. I started to head down to the park. A blinking light on my phone signaled a message and the thought of money coming our way entered my mind. Piles of unanswered messages were stacked by my calendar, a calendar that was filled with unmet goals. While Louise's words echoed in my head that a moment in the park would do me good, David's words echoed louder.

Get to work.

I'd resolved to spend the night in the office. Whatever it took to put the business plan together, show the team I was on their side, and focus on another path. This was the month I had to nab a few venture capitalists, but I also needed to return to my roots. I had to find the courage to return to the youthful risk-taker I once was. Basically, I had to find humility.

I called Shelly to let her know I wouldn't be home. A tough call to make, as even my days at home lately were mired in self-pity. The kids couldn't tell, but Shelly knew. She always knew. We'd learned to understand one another better than we understood ourselves. She wanted me to do what needed to be done both for me and for our family. She also knew family included my employees, and that I had no intention of failing with this family we'd built.

I checked the message. It wasn't money coming in. In fact, it was someone following up on a delayed payment. Since it was after hours, most of these messages couldn't be responded to now, anyway. So I decided to take that walk and maybe even talk to Purple Hat.

"Julie," I said as I passed her desk, "go home. It's after six."

"A few more things, and then I'm gone. You okay?"

"Rough day. But we'll pull it together tomorrow. Thank God there is always a tomorrow."

Otto walked past with a stack of papers and a hard drive on top of the stack. He looked at the keys in my hand assuming I was heading home.

"See boss," Otto said, "I hate to say it, but we're all still here. All of us. I know you have a family, but personally speaking I'd like to someday start a family. Once I signed on to work here I haven't been on more than a couple of dates. I'm always here."

I gave my best "that was inappropriate" stare, but he turned out of frustration and walked on, shaking his head.

"I'm not leaving, Otto," I yelled at his back.

"Jake, you can't let him talk to you like that. It's a power play."

"Yeah, and when he sees me in here an hour from now he'll think he had some influence. I'm taking a walk, and I'll be back. You be out having drinks before I return, okay? Drag Otto with you."

I walked through the park, passing suits with smiles on their faces. Everyone had a smile on their face as if they didn't have a care in the world. Including Purple Hat, who still sat there.

I glanced back at him while I passed afraid he'd been staring, and not only did he stare, he waved again. I shot my hand up and continued on. Independence Hall, gardens, cobbled streets, and sidewalks went by in a blur; I'd walked longer than planned, mind racing with thoughts, options, outs… options of closing down tomorrow and starting over, going back to the basics. But just one investor would put a smile back on my face. Just one. But three or four months before payment unsettled my stomach. That would total almost a full year without income.

I passed the small, two-level brick house where Ben Franklin once lived. I walked near where Thomas Jefferson wrote draft after draft of the Declaration of Independence-the drafts of a document giving me the freedom to make all these choices. But I didn't feel free. I felt trapped. And the trap I'd set for myself. I stopped and bought dinner. An everything bagel just like my daughter Emma liked.

Rounding the corner, I saw Purple Hat throw soft pretzel pieces to the birds. I walked closer to him this time and he said, "Have a seat. You look like you could toss a few words off someone."

I couldn't see his eyes for the face-enveloping sunglasses and the purple Phillies hat covered most of his thinning hair. But I could see his warm smile.

"I've never seen a purple Phillies cap before."

"Well, now you have."

"That really is strange. I saw a blue cap once and even a green one they made up to celebrate a St. Patrick's Day spring training game, but never a purple one. Where'd you get it?"

"It's just a hat that someone gave me years ago." The old man laughed at my question like it was a joke I should understand, but did not get. Then, he turned to look at me through his dark, thick sunglasses.

"Why do you keep squinting, son?"

"I guess it's the bright sunset. I wish it could stay like this all year." I answered watching happy couples and families. I wanted to be home tossing a ball with little Jake. I wanted to look at Emma's homework, and pretend I could solve the math problems.

"You should wear sunglasses like these," he answered.

"Well, those certainly are fancy. And they definitely make a fashion statement."

"I don't have the time to waste trying to make everybody happy. I quit that a long time ago. I shop for things I need, things that are practical. I don't much care to make fashion statements. Well, I don't mind making a statement with the cars I drive. I love cars."

"Really? So do I. Just got into the racing business."

"How is that working for you?"

"Ah, I love it. But nothing is really working for me right now."

He leaned toward me, pointing to his glasses, and lowering his voice asked, "Would you like to try them on?"

"They're definitely unique, but I think I'll pass."

"So, you know me by my purple cap, and I know you by your frown. Strange world, isn't it?" The old man laughed under his breath as he looked up at a feeding squirrel.

"My frown?"

"I call you Frown Man," he crossed one leg over the other. "So Mr. Frown Man, what's your real name?"

"Jacob Edwards," I put out my hand.

He either didn't see or just decided to ignore my offer. "Nobody else in this park wears those fancy clothes and sits on a park bench for lunch every day frowning as much as you."

"How long have you been watching me?"

"Oh, I've been watching you for quite some time now. I like to study people." The man began to rock back and forth on the bench. "So, why the constant frown?"

"Because things have been better in my life, and I don't know how to fix it." I was surprised I'd said that much, but he was right. I could use someone to bounce some words off. The office was too involved and my wife was, well, I didn't need to worry her, yet. "I'm working hard to get a new company up and going, and economic times are difficult."

"Well, son, we're at the bottom of a cycle. You should've been prepared for this because business runs in cycles," he said.

I was taken aback with this comment. Business cycles it seemed to be a theme in my life!

"You know," he continued studying my face for reaction, "people are funny. Kids wonder why adults want them to study history in school. It makes no sense to them. The true value of history doesn't make sense till you get older, much older. That's when you start to understand the old adage 'what comes around, goes around.' Eventually, everything you do in business comes back to you. Good business practices pay off in great reputations. Business mistakes or lapses eventually create bad feelings that are hard to fight." He sounded like he was rehashing a college lecture.

"So what's your name?" I asked, trying again to shake his hand.

"Oh, you can call me Duke," he replied, turning to look at a bird in the tree, again avoiding my handshake.

"You seem to understand business pretty well," I went on. "What kind of experience do you have?"

"Well, I've put more than a few business ventures under my belt. I've been pretty successful at a handful, and I've had my share of problems."

I wondered if I'd stumbled upon one of those eccentric millionaires you read about but never meet: reclusive, successful businessmen who spend their older years wearing funny hats and hanging out in public parks.

"What do you recommend I try?" I asked, and qualified it, "I'm interested in hearing what you have to say. I can't promise I'll take your advice. But nothing I've tried so far seems to work." My chuckling at the end of the sentence was meant to add levity.

"Ask yourself a question," he answered looking me straight in the eye. "Is your glass half full or half empty?"

"Well, I like to think I'm an optimist," I answered. "I never would have come as far as I have unless I believed in myself. Even if I end up changing paths along the way, somehow I always seem to get to my destination."

"Well then, Jacob…it is Jacob, right?"

"Jacob, Jake, whatever."

"Well, Jacob, from where I'm sitting it sounds like your glass is half full and frozen."

"Half full and frozen? I don't get it."

"Think about it. You'll get it. If you make it back here again, we'll talk some more."

Duke stood and stretched. I expected to hear bones crack.

"I have to go. It's not easy to sit on a hard park bench for too long. I prefer soft leather." He rotated one shoulder then the next. "By the way, your suit looks great, but your breath stinks. What was on that bagel?"

I laughed, "Thank you, I think. It was an everything bagel. You should try one."

"Too much garlic and onion," he answered. "Not tomorrow, but the next day bring two bagels: one for each of us. But make them both plain." He walked away.

I imagined him returning to a run down shack, with a hundred cats wandering in and out of sparse rooms, and millions of dollars buried in barrels under his porch.

Then I imagined me returning to an office where everyone still sat at their desks, working, wondering where I'd been, and wondering what my brain was going to come up with to keep this together. In fact, I had devised a few ideas, and it was hard for me to convince myself they were good. A half-full glass, I realized, frozen, was exactly where I was.

When I was a child, my parents gave me all the tools I needed to make that first break. I realized that after I bought my first car with cash. My father once told me, in one of our many late night talks on the porch, "Jake, you gotta figure what you want in this life and find the people who want to go there with you. Just make sure you spend your time with good people."

This memory struck me in the gut when I entered the dark offices expecting to see no one, and my daughter sat behind my desk, obviously on instant messenger chatting with friends.

"Hey Dad."

"Emma? How did you get here? Where are Mommy and Jake?"

"I got a ride with Janie's mom. They had to come into the city to visit her grandmom in the hospital. They're picking me up in an hour or two."

"You still shouldn't be here alone. But I have to say, it's nice to see you sitting there."

"I ran into Louise on her way out. She let me in. Who were you talking to on the bench?"

"You saw me? Why didn't you say something?"

"You looked pretty into the conversation. Looked like a nice guy, but what's the deal with the huge bug-eye glasses?"

"He's a nice man from what I can tell. I just met him, but I feel like I've known him for years."

"Are you going to be real late? I was hoping to hitch a ride home with you."

"I'm going to be all night, maybe."

She put her head on my desk.

"Everything okay?" I asked.

"Sure," she stood, "I just thought I might be able to help get you home sooner, plus I forgot about some homework I need to finish."

"You have dinner?"

"No," she said. "But can we go to that Chinese place on the corner? I can call Janie's mom and have her pick me up there."

"Sweetheart, I don't have time for Chinese. But, let's grab a cheesesteak on the corner, and if you don't tell your mother, we can get a sundae with peanut butter and hot fudge just the way you like it."

"No Daddy, that's just the way you like it."

I called Tracy, Janie's mom, and arranged for her to pick Emma up downstairs.

My family wasn't used to me not being home at night, and the minute I reclaimed my place in the business world things would return to normal. Better than normal.

I focused. Pulling out the financials David dropped off, I put Bob's presentation front and center, and I tackled the first group of investors that I'd meet in a couple days. I took the phone off the hook, threw my cell phone into the back of a drawer, turned off email, and fell into a zone.

The Glass Is
Half Full and Frozen

CHAPTER FOUR

Tuesday, October 4

Checking Account Balance: $449,020

"Jake!"

I snapped my head up to see Louise standing in an absolute panic. A piece of paper that was fastened by drool fell from my lip.

"Jake, I thought you were dead or at least kidnapped."

"What?"

"You have ten messages from your wife that your daughter spent much of the night in the hospital. She was in a car accident last night on the way home."

I jumped to my feet and headed for the door, papers, face, and suit all over the place. She put her hand on my chest.

"Emma is home, completely fine, sprained arm. It's you everyone is worried about. Michaels & Company is waiting to talk to you in the conference room. I can tell them you have an emergency."

My brain scrambled to figure what day it was and why they were here.

"This isn't their meeting day. It's two days from now."

"No, it's tomorrow. But, they have an out-of-town conference tomorrow with another start-up and decided to show a day early to give you a chance. I can tell them you have a family emergency, but they released Emma after a few hours. She's fine. You could do this meeting and head home right afterwards. Why was your cell off?"

"I had it on vibrate. I certainly didn't plan to sleep here. Okay, tell them I need ten more minutes."

"He's been here thirty.

"Buy me some time. I look like death. I need to call home before I do anything."

"I'm dialing for you now. I was not going to let you go into that meeting without first calling your family. Oh, by the way, the banker's name is Andrew Tremmel, and he's been looking around."

While I tried to straighten my jacket, I was shaken from worry, concern, and the feeling I need to be both home for my family and here for my family. I briefly went over what I'd reviewed last night as I brushed my teeth. Thank God I keep a spare set of clothes in the office. I may look like crap, but at least the PowerPoint presentation Bob and the team did was excellent.

I dashed through the door, passing Louise again, my mind racing, reminding me of the days when I'd wake thirty minutes late for classes, sick to my stomach, and wanting to be home. A daddy CEO balancing being here *for* the family and being there *with* the family. Sounds like a book I need to write.

"What should we do about feeding this guy?" Louise asked, without turning.

"Don't worry about it. We still have some sodas and OJ in the refrigerator, don't we? And there's a bagel vendor outside. Except, I don't have any money on me. Emma got me last night for dinner. Oh, Emma, she was still asleep when I called, but Shelly said she is fine."

"I'll be right back with the bagels," she said as she turned.

"How do I look?" I asked her as I straightened my tie.

"Tired," Louise smiled and said nothing else, her silence speaking volumes.

"Louise, when I hired you, I said you needed to be 80% administrative assistant, 10% mother and 10% drill sergeant," I smiled as I held the door for her. "You always seem to know exactly what I need."

She squeezed my arm. "Why don't you go in there and do what you do best. Get that man's checkbook."

I stopped as my hand reached for the door to the conference room. I took a second to see in my mind's eye the outcome of this meeting, a very positive outcome. I pushed out my chest and took a deep breath as I opened the door.

Inside, Otto sat with Andrew, the two quite involved in conversation.

"Good morning, Andrew," I said in the same practiced voice with which I'd delivered the Wharton speech. "You'll have to excuse the delay. I didn't know to expect you. I'm Jacob Edwards, founder and CEO. Welcome to our company." I extended my hand.

"Morning, Otto," I turned to him. "How are you?"

"Great, Jake, thanks."

After his reprimand last night, I felt more like the student in the principal's office than the boss. Once I knocked this crisis out, I knew I'd have another with Otto.

"It's good to meet you, too," Mr. Tremmel said. He was the kind of man that walked into a room and commanded attention.

"You've got quite a facility here," he said, studying the molding on the ceiling of the conference room. "Of course, I've heard a lot about you, and I've had the chance to talk with Otto. And I met with one of your technical guys earlier. Bob, I believe. You have a great staff and a nice office." His attention again shifted to the trappings of the conference room.

"I'm looking forward to hearing why you feel we should invest in your company and your people…and you, of course," he snickered.

I wasn't quite up for this. He rattled me, and I'm not easily rattled. He had control, commanding an authority his boss paid for. What was more unnerving was how cool Otto appeared. I know he represented us well, and he saved face for me. But he seemed to know that, too.

"I'm certainly anxious to talk to you," I turned to Otto. "Would you mind giving Mr. Tremmel and me a few minutes alone?"

"Thank you, you were very helpful." Mr. Tremmel and Otto shook hands.

"My pleasure," Otto answered. "You're in the hands of the best now. I wouldn't be here otherwise."

During our meeting I munched on a bagel to prevent passing out from starvation, but Andrew declined. It was a good hour and half later when Mr. Tremmel and I finished our meeting. Bob, Julie, and Elaine were in the reception area heading to lunch.

"Hey, guys." I smiled at them reassuringly. "I understand you've met Mr. Tremmel of Michaels & Company?"

Mr. Tremmel interrupted, "Jake, you have quite a team here."

"I'm proud of them," I nodded more to them than him. "They all share my excitement. And I'm sure we're all looking forward to the opportunity to work for you and your firm. In fact, we'd consider it an honor."

"Start achieving some of the goals outlined for me, and you'll be set," Mr. Tremmel said. "It was nice meeting all of you." We shook hands and he turned for the door.

"We'll be in touch," he said over his shoulder. Famous last words, the words that make us cringe in every profession, relationship, and situation.

Everyone waited for me to sum up the meeting.

"Relax, guys. I think we did great. I'm not sure what you all told him, but it must have been good; by the time I got started he knew most of the answers. I gave a simple elevator pitch, talked about each of you and your roles, and reviewed our goals. From what I gather, they're considering several companies, but I feel pretty safe that if we can pull off a good meeting with their board, we'll get a letter of intent."

"So this wasn't the meeting, then?" asked Bob.

"No. He wanted to meet us and see what we look like in action. It'll give him some perspective. Now we just need to make sure we put together a killer presentation for his partners."

"How about lunch, crew?" Julie asked. "Jake can get the first round of water."

"You guys go," I said, "I have to head home. I'll see you this afternoon."

On the way to my car, I called Shelly. She was near tears

seemingly more upset now than when I spoke with her before. I dabbed at my eyes crossing the bridge into Jersey. I was ashamed, embarrassed, and completely without the words to fix this.

Later that afternoon, little Jake sat on my lap as I sat beside Emma's bed. She watched TV while I sat there. I tried to talk with her, but I wasn't saying the right things.

"I'm proud of you. You're treating this like a champ."

"Thanks."

"You know I'm sorry. If I'd been here to help," I stopped myself. "Things will change soon. I swear. I don't make empty promises, do I?"

She finally looked at me.

"No. We just miss you."

"And I miss you all terribly."

"Dad, remember that racecar accident you had when you did some trial runs? I feel like I did that last night without a helmet. No fun."

I wasn't the kind of father that spent weeks and weeks away from family and made false promises that things would improve. Before this business start-up, I'd spoiled them and myself by taking long vacations, spending every evening at home and some late mornings, with occasional work binges where for a few days I might be sparse. This was the longest run ever.

I kissed her on the forehead as my cell rang. She grabbed it from my hand and opened it. "Hello?"

I tried to take it, but she turned her head.

"He's with my brother right now but can call you later. Bye." She clicked the phone shut and tossed it back.

"Someone from your office. I know I'm probably in trouble for that, but Mom's on my side." Jake laughed and ran out of the room yelling to his mother that Emma had got into trouble.

"You're not in trouble. I should let you answer all my calls."

"Going back to work?"

"I have to. Sorry."

"Dad, can't you just hang out here today. What can you do at work this afternoon that will change things?"

Get to work.

I looked in my daughter's eyes, my wife's eyes, and I said, "Nothing, baby. I'm home for the day."

I sat to have a sandwich with Shelly, and I promised her as well that this would change. I told her about the investor meeting, and that Emma was now screening my calls, which could change everything.

My cell rang again, and it was Julie. A delivery had been made that wasn't approved by either of us but was addressed to Bob. I gave her permission to accept, unknowing at the time the cost and nature of the purchase. That package would make tomorrow, and the next several days, quite interesting.

I also asked what the nature of the earlier call was. She hadn't called. But she had given Andrew Tremmel my number as he had a question regarding our financials. Emma had hung up on my potential investor. I would clean it all up first thing tomorrow morning. For the remainder of that day my only concern was my family.

THE GLASS IS
HALF FULL AND FROZEN

CHAPTER FIVE

Wednesday, October 5

Checking Account Balance: $446,502

(after the COD for the package yesterday)

On my way back into the office I looked up recent received calls
and re-dialed the number Emma had hung up on.

"Andrew Tremmel."

"Hi, Andrew. Jacob Edwards. Sorry I missed your call
yesterday."

"Quite an answering service you have there, Jacob."

"Yeah, well, someday she's going to be running this country. I
apologize."

"Don't. It was very funny. Jacob, the partners pointed out a small
problem they'd like to work around. It seems your financial statement
doesn't reflect recent transactions. They were asking if it was possible to
get our records current."

I was cornered. Our records stopped a couple months ago when we could justify zero income. How were we supposed to explain to an investor that we didn't have a single client?

"Yes, Andrew, that is an issue for us. I'm actually working with the team and my accountant to get everything up to date. Perhaps we can meet at some point and go over that particular plan?" I hoped that would buy me a week or two. After all, we'd only met yesterday morning.

"Okay, can I call at the end of the day to schedule that after you talk with your team?" He was pushy and sounded distrusting. Not that I could blame him for the latter.

"Why don't you give me till the end of next week?" I asked, trying not to sound desperate.

"How about next Wednesday? I'll talk to you the very first thing that morning." He answered as he hung up. I stared at the phone for a moment before I put it down. Who did this guy think he was, deciding when and how I would do my work? And the mistrust, well, I had to admit that could be justified. After all, I was hoping I could figure a way he wouldn't look at those reports.

As I turned to head to the office I saw Duke smiling and shaking his head. He was evidently listening to the conversation. I plopped beside him.

"Boy," he said, "you got a mess. And you didn't meet me for

breakfast like you promised."

"I'm not keeping many promises these days. And I thought we said tomorrow. But, I'm glad to see you. I could use the conversation."

"I've got things to do, friend. But you need a moment. A moment to yourself is worth a month of therapy. Don't waste it."

He walked away. I started to walk away as well. But instead I remained, cleared my mind, and considered the beauty of this park and of the smiles on the faces of those around. I replayed the joy of spending an afternoon with my family. I reminded myself that the feeling of promise would return someday. I'd join those walking in the park, smiling, thankful for the opportunity to make choices, fail, and start over. I also determined, once I broke out of this cycle, if I saw a guy or gal like me, the Frown Man, sitting on a bench, I'd be there to provide the support they needed. After twenty minutes, I entered the building with a little more spring in my step.

"Thanks for your patience with me yesterday, Julie. Emma's accident and my not being there really screwed me up. How are things here?"

"Positive. Everyone is quite positive."

"The delivery still here?"

"Yes, and I have the invoice. It's astronomical and charged to the office account."

She handed it to me. Anger shot through my every vein. How could Bob do this? I went to his office where he was plugging a state-of-the-art monitor in to his system.

"Hi Jake."

"Bob. We didn't approve that purchase."

"Not yet you haven't, but it was a necessary purchase. I got the latest high tech monitor available. It's got a 21-inch flat screen that's going to look great on my desk and goes well with the new offices. I ordered another two for the other guys."

"It's an unauthorized purchase. Nobody does that in our organization. You have a clear budget established. This is the only company I know of where everyone not only gets input into the budget, but we draft it as a team."

"Right, boss. But I'm almost finished working the kinks out of version 2.0, and I figured this was as good a time as any to set up some new equipment before we get slammed with new customers."

"Is something wrong with your old monitor?" I interrupted.

"No, except that it's really pretty small and hard to work with."

"This is on our account, Bob. A business account that's being closely examined right now."

"I felt like you trusted me to do my job, Jake. Maybe I'm wrong? Maybe I'm getting mixed messages from all this restructuring."

He turned and continued the installation process. Keeping myself from making an inappropriate comment, I walked from his office.

Otto walked past. "Oh, Jake. You're here."

"How's it going Otto?"

"Um, got a minute?"

We went to my office where a stack of papers had appeared on my desk and messages were posted all over my monitor. If I hadn't taken that refreshing moment in the park, I might have walked back out. Topping the list of messages was one Julia had taken from the building landlord. Partial rent payments weren't enough anymore, and he was giving thirty days to get up to date. Obviously prime real estate, I feared this would happen. I had just hoped his books were as behind as ours.

"Jake," Otto said, "I'm still concerned. I enjoyed the meeting we had last month, but honestly I think we all pulled together without you. I hate to sound critical all the time, but I'm concerned. You realize Andrew Tremmel called me twice yesterday afternoon with questions? I tried to turn him to you, but he said you were unavailable. This isn't my job. I'm not your assistant."

It took every bit of maturity not to tell him what I was really thinking at that moment. Deal with the message and do not kill the messenger I had to tell myself.

"Honestly, do you think I don't realize I'm stretched too thin?"

"I know you realize it. But if you don't focus, we're going to crash. Together, yes, but a crash nonetheless."

"I'm struggling, Otto. Not just with the company, but with your attitude. And I'm not sure I feel all that insulted by it. That's the thing. I should be insulted. But," and I didn't want to say it, "you might be right on target. However, if you want to be a business leader, it's not always just the message, it's also the method. You can be direct with me, but as your career progresses you have to learn diplomacy to win the war, not just the individual battles."

"Jake, I'm not against you. I'm more on your side than you know. But if we crashed, and I didn't say what was on my mind, I'd feel as much at fault as anyone."

"Thanks for your honesty. I promise I'm working to make all the necessary changes."

He walked out, not inspired, but at least he knew I was listening.

Because of Otto's resolve and honesty, I had a moment of inspiration. Just like the old days, I made three decisions from my gut and decided to move forward with them unquestioningly. One was to fire the least effective team player, which was no longer me. Second was to move this facility, which fit with the third decision to include my family in day to day activity.

I paged Julie.

"I need an employee termination form, please."

"I saw Otto walk out perturbed," she replied. "I can't believe he'd quit though."

"This isn't a voluntary termination."

Thirty minutes later I'd filled out the paperwork and had Julie and Bob join me in my office.

Bob sat in front of me; he started to squirm. He obviously knew something was wrong, but seemed oblivious to the real problem.

"Bob," I began, measuring my words. "Do you remember what I told you the first day you started working here? What we repeated in our recent team meeting?" I watched for a reaction. "Do you remember what I said about the way teams work?"

"The weakest link mantra. We're only as good as our weakest point?"

"We're struggling to survive, and you spent over two thousand dollars on new monitors."

"So that's what this is all about?" he interrupted. "I can't work in the middle ages. If you want me to do my job, you're going to have to at least provide me with good tools to work with. Plus, you're sending the wrong message, Jake. I don't know if you want me in control of my job or if you want to micromanage me."

"Bob, I'm not sure we're on the same page here. I can't afford to buy every little convenience any employees would like. Plus, I would call a flat screen a luxury this company cannot justify. Even more than that, you spent company money without permission. Before you spend company money, you must clear it with the budget team."

"I really don't think either one of us has the time to discuss every little purchase I make. You're never here, anyway." His arrogant answer, and the fact that I'd spent the night here while my daughter spent part of the night in the hospital, forced the issue. Negative attitudes spread like viruses. One person takes a stand and starts pushing. If nothing happens, the rest of the crowd follows. Otto approached me directly; Bob went behind all our backs.

"I would have told you not to purchase the monitor. Not right now, anyway."

"And I would have probably quit."

"Bob, maybe that's what needs to happen here," I said, keeping with my conviction to do this swiftly and without question. "Why don't you pack your things up and leave."

"Are you firing me?" he asked defiantly.

"Yes, Bob, I'm firing you. I'll have accounting cut you a check for two weeks, although I'm tempted to keep it to cover the cost of the monitors."

It suddenly hit him. His eyes dropped to the floor. He looked like a scolded child.

"Bob, you're a good CTO. You have the potential to go places. But you need to remember, there are other people in this world besides yourself. As soon as you learn to work with the team, you're going to make a great employee. Right now, we can't afford your mistakes. As you know, this is not the first issue. You missed the projection of when we'd finish version 2.0. I don't know why you missed the projection, but it was another setback for us. These purchases are an even more serious setback."

If he'd apologized, taken responsibility, or even offered something then things might have turned out differently.

He answered somewhere between a moan and a challenge. "Anderson and Associates called me the other day to offer me a job from an old resume. At least they have clients."

I started to offer advice but caught myself. He obviously wasn't interested in anything but saving face.

"And I won't need your severance pay. Keep it to help pay for the monitors." He stormed toward the door. "At least the other programmers will appreciate what I've done."

Julie and I sat quietly for a moment then she said, "You did the right thing. You sent a good message, and you got a potential crisis under control."

"Thanks. Send the check in the mail."

I knew I *had* done the right thing. It was one of those moments everybody watched. Somehow the boss is always the last person to know when there's trouble in the ranks, but when he finds out, everybody sits back and watches how he'll react. It's like being a surgeon. When you discover cancer, you have to decide if you want to sit back and hope for a miracle, or dive in immediately and cut it out before it spreads. Bob's feelings may have been hurt, but the rest of the team would go home tonight knowing I had their best interests in mind. It felt good to have the certainty I'd done something right.

"I have three other very qualified applicants waiting for that job," Julie said.

I took a deep breath and smiled. Julie was on top of things and nobody could ask for anyone better than Louise: both were models of efficiency.

"I really am glad you're on my side," I told her as Louise entered. "But we need to hold off filling his position. No more expenses that we cannot justify. Oh, and I have some other news, Julie. We're moving. I need to schedule a team meeting for early next week. It's time we climb back to the top instead of hanging for dear life at the bottom."

"Where will we go?" Louise asked.

"The basement of my house."

The Glass is
Half Full and Frozen

CHAPTER SIX

Wednesday, October 5 - evening

Checking Account Balance: $406,502

For the remainder of the day, the office was busy. Julie and Louise kept the move a secret, but Bob made his release an issue. The office team professionals paid him little attention, outside the occasional word of encouragement. We worked hard that day, and I made sure everyone left the office on time. I told them after the weekend there would be double duty asked of them.

At home, Emma wandered around the yard dribbling a basketball with one hand. The arm was healing, but she was still pretty sore.

"Hey, toss it here."

She threw me the ball, and I tossed it with one arm missing the basket by a mile.

She rebounded and shot with one arm, a perfect swish.

"Mom and Jake are heading out to his school for a mother-son thing."

"So I've heard. You wanna take a drive for a father-daughter night out?"

She smiled. "So you're home, huh?"

"I think you'll be seeing a lot of me from now on. And everybody else as well."

"What do you mean?"

"Hop in. Let's drive."

"Only if we play Linkin Park and you let me shift."

It was a gorgeous night. For part of the drive we didn't talk. We just enjoyed the music on the radio and the cool autumn air on our faces. We drove toward the college strip in the city and passed one of my old college hangouts. I slowed down to watch the kids studying over coffee.

"I spent many late nights studying in the corner there, near the guitar player." The guitar player's job was to exist in the subconscious of the students and writers. He was our white noise.

"Let's go in, Dad. Looks cool."

I ordered a decaf iced café mocha for myself and a hot chocolate for Emma.

We took a seat near the guitarist in this packed house. Emma studied his playing as I surveyed the room. Three guys in the corner worked feverishly on a project. Their eyes said they had all the answers; nothing could stop them. I felt a tinge of envy creep in. I wanted, for a moment, unrelenting assurance that I, too, was unstoppable. After all, I once was. I knew it then and therefore it was true.

"Do you mind if I join you?" a girl in her late teens pointed at a chair across from us.

"No, help yourself." I smiled, thinking that in any other setting that would have looked like a pick up. But coffee shop patrons were different. There were no boundaries. You could turn to the table next to yours and strike up a conversation any time. If you saw someone that looked interesting, it was perfectly normal to walk up and say hi.

"You're Jacob Edwards, aren't you?" she asked as she pulled the chair out.

Emma looked at me with the same undisguised amazement with which I looked at the young woman.

"You did a lecture at school a few days ago," she explained, "I was really impressed by what you said."

"Cool," Emma said.

"Oh," I laughed, adding, "I was beginning to think you were a psychic."

She smiled back.

"My daughter, Emma."

"Hi." She reached for Emma's hand, and then shook mine. "I'm Beth. Do you mind if I ask you a few questions?"

It felt good to have a young student look up to me, especially with my daughter in attendance. This was good.

"I don't mind at all."

"Is it really as easy as you made it sound the other day? Because, to be honest, I'm really scared. Nobody in my family ever made it to college. My parents own a farm in western Pennsylvania. I came here on a scholarship, and I'm about to graduate. They expect me to be a big success and all, but, I dunno."

I wanted to say something that would point her in the right direction, but I wasn't sure I knew what that was anymore. But like my meeting with David, and with Andrew, and the morning I spoke to her class, something instinctual took over and words poured from my mouth.

"You won't make it." I began. She shifted nervously in her chair, and I had Emma's full attention as well. "It isn't about reaching the top; it's about moving up a step or two every day. Don't believe you have to be number one. That isn't the goal. The goal is to do your very best. And the victory doesn't come at the end of the road: It comes at the end of the day when you know you've done your best. Learn to savor the process rather than the conclusion, and you'll do fine. Celebrate the little victories."

The three guys at the end table stopped working and turned to listen to me. Emma grinned with pride. I tried not to gloat.

"The most important thing is to be sure you've charted your path. Know where you want to go, and have a plan to get there. If you follow an accurate roadmap to success and make progress every day, you'll have plenty of reason to celebrate. And the day you die, you'll still have plenty of untraveled road left ahead of you, a journey someone else will pick up and continue in your honor."

As I finished, I wished I had recorded that. It sounded like the kind of stuff I needed to hear morning after morning.

"So I don't have to be a success," she said.

"I didn't say that." I stopped her. "You don't have to be incredibly rich to be happy. All it takes is motion in the right direction. Knowing you're on course and moving is the success you hope to achieve. All that other stuff is icing on the cake."

"How do you know you're on the right track?"

"That's the ten million dollar question. You have to make your share of mistakes in order to know what to avoid. You have to watch others and pay attention in class so you can avoid the mistakes of others. And you'll have to get used to your share of failures. The point is, unless you give up, even the failures are steps in the right direction stepping stones that teach you what to avoid. They're the pain we all feel in order to grow. They're the obstacle course that builds character, and character builds successful people."

I was tempted to tell them about the problems I now faced. I wondered if it would encourage them or make them lose respect for the lessons I'd tried to teach them. It would definitely be therapeutic, but I decided against it.

"Guys, I'd love to stay and chat, but I have a very busy day ahead of me tomorrow and I better get going. Besides, my daughter is freaking out here. She's never heard me talk like this." And she'd never seen me get this much attention.

"Unless we are at the track and you're spinning out of control in your race car, like usual." Everyone laughed at Emma's comment.

We got up as the guys in the corner thanked me. Emma even stopped to talk to one of the younger college guys wearing a Flyers jersey, and if I didn't know better, I'd swear she was flirting. But I motioned her onward, and we left the café.

On the way home she asked questions about business and success, and she related it to things her coach mentioned in terms of basketball.

"And," she laughed, "it was just like the time at the track when all of two or three people requested your autograph."

It was a good night. The best I'd had in a long time.

My head on my pillow that night, I thought of Bob and how this probably wasn't the same night he experienced. I felt for him, but he'd put our company even more in the hole, and I again reaffirmed to myself that I'd done the right thing.

I spent the weekend playing with my family, trying to forget the business. The next week, the move into my own home crowded my thoughts. And, the man in the Purple Hat was sorely missed.

THE GLASS IS
HALF FULL AND FROZEN

CHAPTER SEVEN

Monday, October 10

Checking Account Balance: $397,882

I woke up at 5:30 a.m. I'd planned to meet Duke for breakfast and a chat to kick start my day. I rushed around the house like a teenager readying for a date. I arrived at the park to little traffic. I almost jogged as the sunrise and light frost (but a warm day was forecasted) provided exactly the invigorating atmosphere I'd hoped for. It's strange how nature can give us what we need most. More than money, more than perhaps love, close attention to nature is an unquestionably uplifting experience.

The guy at the deli smiled and asked if I wanted the usual.

"No, not today. I need two coffees. One straight, one wimpy. Extra cream and sugar. And two plain bagels."

"Plain? You're not a plain bagel guy."

"Unless you start serving breath mints with the everything bagels, I might have changed my routine."

"Breath mints. Not a bad idea, pal. Extra quarter for them, and I toss a couple in the bag. Not a bad idea."

As I took my bagels and coffee tray, I noticed all the Phillies memorabilia on the wall. I had seen it before, but this time I looked closer.

"Have you ever seen a purple Phillies cap?" I asked over my shoulder.

"No, never. And I've seen everything that has to do with the Phillies. Why would they make a purple hat? This ain't Barney's team."

I nodded in agreement and wished him a good one.

I arrived at the park around seven o'clock, and found Duke sitting on the bench feeding the pigeons.

"How's it going?" I asked as I sat down to flailing wings and the scattering of birds and loose feathers.

"Well, it was going fine until you scared off the birds."

"Sorry to disturb your friends."

He pointed at the bag, and I removed our coffees.

"And two plain bagels," I announced triumphantly as I handed him one.

"Your breath smells much better today. Does that mean you've decided to clean up your act?"

I wasn't sure if the question was rhetorical, but his insistent stare told me he awaited an answer.

"I don't think my real problems are solved no matter how my breath is. I'm ready to do whatever it takes to get my affairs in order," I answered humbly.

"You mean to say clean up your act. 'Get my affairs in order' makes it sound like there isn't much to work on."

"Okay, my life's a mess, and I need to clean up my act," I conceded.

"So, what's your roadmap?" he asked, again waiting for my answer. His question sounded as if he'd heard me at the coffee shop last night.

"I guess I want to feel successful again. But it seems I keep running into obstacles. Friday, I had to fire a guy whose only goal was looking after himself." I went on to tell him about the situation with Bob and the meeting the team would have within the hour.

Duke stared at the ground in front of him for a long time before he answered.

"Jake," he started slowly, "my guess is you're going to have several of your employees quit on you before the end of the week."

"What?" I was surprised. This was the first negative, truly negative, comment Duke had made to me. "I'm making it clear to them things are going to change, that I am taking back control of the company, and we will push forward. Why wouldn't they be excited about that?"

"That's not what you're telling them," he answered defiantly. "Your leadership leads them to work in your basement, and you expect them to be excited at the prospect? Would you continue to work for a man like that?"

It made sense. One reason for the quiet mode around the office was that they all wondered if I was going to fire them, or if the company was about to fold and they'd lose their jobs anyway.

"You're right again," I said, feeling defeated. "I'm screwing this all up. How is this happening?"

"It isn't about who's right; it's about figuring out what's right and getting busy doing it."

"But what can I do now?" I asked. I felt like a parent trying to figure out how to raise teenagers. How many employees had turned in resumes at other companies, and how many planned to do so?

"You can accept responsibility for being a bumbling oaf," he laughed. "There's a big difference between being aggressive and being assertive. You've proven to them you're the authority because you sign the paychecks, but you aren't giving them reason to respect you. And without respect, there is no team: just a bunch of scared individuals looking out for their survival.

"You can stay in control while showing concern and empathy for their needs. Tell them what's in your heart. They need to know how important each of them is to you, and how much their personal input and drive means to your company. In today's meeting, why don't you have them each explain their own personal goals within the company and in their private lives? Show them how your company can help make their own objectives a reality."

Suddenly, as if he realized he should have been elsewhere all along, Duke got up. "Gotta go, picking up a new car today! Thanks for the bagel. Your breath cleans up nicely when you do the right thing." He turned and walked away.

I spent fifteen more minutes alone arranging thoughts, and then I headed straight for the conference room for what I knew would be one of the last meetings in this amazing office building.

Everyone was there when I arrived, as solemn as they had been month before. I now translated the uncertainty in their eyes. I'd mistaken this look the previous day for focus, when in fact it was doubt.

"I'm sure most of you realize I've been paying the bills out of my own personal savings. Just yesterday, I transferred money to our company account to make sure we have cash on hand for the next few months. While that should make you feel confident, you also need to know some of our current costs."

Few looked me in the eye.

"The landlord of this building has decided we're too much of a credit risk and refuses to renew our lease. We're going to have to find another home for our company. I've decided, for now, I'm going to set us up in the basement of my house."

And with that, everyone looked me straight in the eye.

"It's only a half hour drive from here, and there's plenty of room to work. No more city parking and wage tax." Everyone smiled. It was like getting a raise, but quickly reality set in. "We call ourselves a start-up, and it's time we act like it. I'm going to show up in Chamber meetings and other marketing venues to spread the word we're ready for business. If any of you have any friends or relatives that can use our services, let me know. I'd like to send them a promo package.

"I want you to know if you decide you can't work for a company that runs from a basement, I understand. You're all part of this team, and I need each of you. But you should think this through. Once we start the move forward, we'll go full throttle and nobody will have time to doubt."

The silence was deafening, so I took Duke's advice one step further.

"I never had any intention of making you feel your jobs were on the line or your performance was anything less than stellar. We're going through rough times, but I feel confident we're going to pull through. And the only reason I say that without hesitation is because of all of you.

Every one of you is a winner, and I'm proud of our association."

One of the newest team members, Kathy Lindley, smiled, mostly out of relief. She has a son in college and a daughter a junior in high school. She certainly didn't need the stress I'd caused.

"I told every one of you we are a team, and then, when the going got rough, I acted like I was king and nobody but me knew what was best. That was wrong and probably an act of desperation. And you, Otto, showed me that as much as anyone. I thank you for your individual leadership."

He nodded. He had what I once had. Why this guy didn't go out on his own was a mystery to me. I looked to him for the confidence in us that even I needed.

"I want to hear what each of you has to say. In fact, as we aim our company toward the future, I want to be sure that future is the future each of you wants."

I then had Louise hand out pads of paper and pens to each person in the room. I asked them to write five personal goals. Once they finished, I asked them to list five goals they saw for themselves as related to the company.

"Would anybody like to share anything on these lists?" I asked, expecting silence.

"I'd like to keep my coffee breaks to the 15 minutes I'm supposed to take," one of the women said. Everybody laughed.

"I guess that means I need to spend less time smoking in the restroom," one of the tech guys chimed in. These were all serious confessions and real substantial goals. The laughter was more from relief of feeling open to talk than the humor of stealing company time for extra long breaks.

"I want to work like I own this company," another said.

"Well, you do," I answered. "Each of you is the real owner. When we succeed, we'll all succeed, because there's no doubt in my mind there isn't one of you unwilling to make it happen."

We talked a bit more about goals, and agreed that each of us should post our goals and our personal mission statement on our desks. As a team, we would take responsibility to help each other reach those goals.

"My personal goal, as it relates to the company," I offered as we started to wrap things up, "is to make one hundred contacts and sell at least twenty-five corporate clients within the next six months. Our main problem is, as was pointed out, I'm depending on a shaky venture capitalist climate. Now, I'm refocusing on customers. I'm going to post a chart in my office and list customers as they sign on. I welcome any of you to hold me accountable to that goal."

As they left the room, they stared into my eyes as they lined up to shake my hand. It was the kind of stare reserved for a close friend, a partner, a teammate. And I smiled as I stared back. They'd forgotten about my basement and concentrated on saving money to build this company.

Louise followed me into my office after the meeting.

"So, about that holding you accountable," she said with a grin. "How did that conversation with Andrew Tremmel go?"

"Oh, right. We need to put together a financial statement that brings us current."

Louise raised her eyebrows, "Are you sure that's wise? All we can show for the past few months is money we've spent getting organized. There's no income to show."

"I realize that," I said trying to sound confident, "but every company has to invest in start-up costs to get going. Plus, I'm hoping to depend less on them as time goes by."

"Jake, you're talking to the lady that organizes all your expenses, remember? If something doesn't happen pretty quickly here, we're going to go broke. You don't have much of a bank account left to depend on."

"I know, but he wants a report and if I tell him no, we lose them for certain. Just put it all down on paper." I found myself looking for answers. "We have to be honest with Tremmel. If we can drum up business before the meeting with his bosses, we might be able to pull it off."

Louise got up and walked around my desk, putting her hand on my shoulder. "We're right behind you," she said as she squeezed my shoulder. "We're going to make this thing work, one way or another."

I reached up and patted her hand. "Thank you. It's not always easy sitting at the top. Sometimes it feels more like I'm a target than a leader. And once I post my list of twenty-five clients, I will be a target."

"Well, nobody can accuse you of not following your own business advice."

Oh, if you only knew, I thought.

"You know, Louise. I think our cup is certainly half-full. And I think it's beginning to thaw just a bit."

"You and your jargon," she shook her head and left the room. But before this ordeal was over, everyone in this office would forever understand, as I now did, how our glasses are often half-full and frozen.

I made a point of going to the coffee shop on my way home that night. I found a quiet corner and read through the goals of those employees who provided copies. There were a few whose goals were unrealistic but most seemed well within our reach. As I looked them over, I noticed an underlying thread. Everybody wanted, rather they needed, to know they could count on their job. They had plans, and their lives would be inconvenienced if I expected them to revolve around my whims. Job security was key, and as a CEO I knew this. It comes with hiring employees and asking that they give their all.

A female acoustic player strummed as I thought about how job security has nothing to do with money. It wasn't about how much money we had in the bank or how much we planned to make. Money is a by-product of being in business. That's true when you're making a lot, and it's true when resources are low. But business isn't about money: it's about customers. As long as we had a long list of customers planning to continue doing business with us, we all had job security. The money would come, the salaries and bills would be paid, only if customers were found and retained.

My next morning goal was to get busy on my chart of 100 calls, hoping for 25 corporate clients within six months. There are around 24 weeks in six months, which meant I had to average one client per week. By averages more of them would pile in near the end, once the momentum started, but only if I could get a good solid start moving up front. I figured it could take at least 200 actual in-person meetings within the six-month period. At that point I figured 25, at least, would be paying customers. Also, I had to make my first call be to Alan Volteer. I really appreciate my relationship with Alan because he is one of the rare people who always returns calls. Now, I owe him a call and out of mutual respect, he will be my first call of the day.

During dinner I explained to the family how the basement office would work, hoping their quality of life would not be affected, or if it was, maybe improved. I invited them all to help with arranging the office space, and Emma spoke for everyone when she said, "Dad, we all want to see more of you, but for that kind of work we need to be on the payroll."

I considered actually giving them some of what we'd save giving up the office. As they quieted, and as the conversation switched to other issues, the view of Philly from my office came to mind. At that moment, I vowed to get that view back someday.

THE GLASS IS
HALF FULL AND FROZEN

CHAPTER EIGHT

Tuesday, October 11

Checking Account Balance: $368,990

I found Duke waiting for me in the park that morning.

"So, how did it go?" he asked, smiling as I tiptoed between pigeons and popcorn. They rustled, but they didn't fly away. Day by day, little by little, I seemed to figure things out.

"It went very well," I answered handing him a cup of coffee. "I think we're on the right path now, in a new company."

"You can start being a team now rather than just theorizing about it."

"It does feel good," I said, for once feeling a bit of relief.

"Now, you can show them you really plan to make things happen. You made a few promises of your own, didn't you?"

It was as if Duke had been in the meeting; he seemed to know the answers to his own questions.

"Yes, I promised to get twenty-five corporate clients within the next six months." I sat up like a student at the foot of a sage who had just answered the most complicated riddle in history, but his face changed into disappointment.

"Sounds like a lofty goal. You better stay busy if you plan on making it."

"I'm going to spend every free moment trying to drum up business. Everybody's been asked to hold me accountable; I want to feel the pressure of knowing this business depends on me and my team and not investment bankers."

Duke looked me straight in the eyes, my reflection shined in those large sunglasses.

"What happens if you fail?"

I never even considered that option.

"I don't know," I stated, lowering my voice.

"Well, you can't fail," he said turning back to the birds. "Not as long as you're giving it your best. Falling short of a goal while doing your best to achieve it is not cause for shame. Not getting there because you did nothing is where shame begins."

This time he got up without saying goodbye. The birds flew in every direction; a couple nearly clipped my head. Over his shoulder, as he walked away, he announced, "See you here at six one week from today."

Six in the morning? As he walked out of sight and out of my voice range, I calculated I'd have to get up at 4:30 to arrive at that hour. I doubted he'd get his coffee and bagel at six in the morning.

I wondered for a moment, as the old man walked away, why he meant so much to me. Moreover, I feared one day he wouldn't appear. Would there come a day when we could discuss life, his life, and not our business lives? I wanted to learn about his life, his loves, and his love of cars at least I know we have that in common. Having been so focused on myself, I didn't even ask him about his new car.

He turned a corner. An urge to chase after him and see where he lived quickly dissipated.

"Morning, Louise. Do me a favor, please," I said as I passed her desk without even looking. "Get me a list of the top five hundred corporations in the Philly area. Be sure it's listed by gross income and not just number of employees." I talked louder as the distance between us stretched. From the corner of my eye I saw Otto watch. "I need names, phone numbers, and mailing addresses. You can probably buy the list online, but if you can't then get it from any list broker in town."

"You got it, boss."

I yearned to work one-on-one with buyers and convince them we were the best choice. I visually put myself in the driver's seat of a race car, getting that adrenaline rush of the green flag. I was ready to make lap after lap, getting past the yellow flags, until we reached the checkered flag of each goal.

At Julie's office I said, "Morning, Julie. I need our graphics people to make up a sharp promotional package that can go out immediately." Then I added loud enough for everyone to hear, "We're going to make this happen!" In the hall I also announced to anyone that would listen, "My eleven year old daughter and six year old son are on payroll at this moment, sweeping your new office floors. You think this place is something, wait until you see their artwork."

I expected to have a list of hot prospects ready to go by tomorrow morning, but I didn't want to wait. I learned early on that the hardest step to cold calling was getting that first call made. Once momentum builds, it's easy to stay on track. Accessing my computer address files, I searched for possible prospects. There were several cards I had picked up at local meetings and parties, and more than a few businesses that would remember me from my previous company associations. For that matter, I'd stayed in contact with almost all of my previous clients. While they knew I had this business underway, I hadn't prodded them for contacts. They knew from my past history that assistance within the network reaps rewards for all involved. Every time I've given something away, I've received ten times that amount in return. It works both ways.

All I needed to do at this point was to give some solid prospects the heads-up that my package was on the way. I pulled up the first name on my prospects list and made the first call.

"Hi, Mike. Jacob Edwards here. How's it going?" After exchanging pleasantries I said, "Mike, I'm calling to let you know I'm busy putting together a new company that can offer some practical, cost-effective answers to some of the obstacles you might be facing. In the next week, you'll be receiving our information package. Then, I would like to call and set a time to learn more about your company and see how I can have a positive affect on your future."

The product we offered was practical *and* cost effective. I knew I could count on a large percentage of sales once they received our package and a follow-up call. In some cases, I might be asked to make a presentation to a purchasing committee, and some companies would ask that I follow up with specific details. I might have to do a bit of negotiating, but overall, the process was streamlined. I had a product they needed, and since I'd pre-screened my prospects, I knew they had the money to buy it. So, all I had to do was convince them that we could deliver in a timely, efficient way.

My speakerphone buzzed.

"What's up, Otto?"

"I figured you were hitting the calls hard today. I had a thought that we should offer lifetime upgrades to these first customers."

"Great idea. How long until we're ready to roll version 2.0?"

"Two weeks, max."

"I'll spread the upgrade word. It gives us testing freedom and the referrals will pour in. Thanks, Otto. How's the training program for this version going? If we get customers, or rather when we get customers, we'll need to roll out the information."

"We're on it. The move will make things interesting."

"Believe me, I know. Thanks again."

That exchange made me feel like a businessman. I didn't even need to get a customer today to get the euphoria of running my own life after a conversation like that.

Why I hadn't started this months ago, I couldn't remember. But my intuition had returned. I kept seeing Duke and, from behind those sunglasses, his look of approval. David would nod in agreement at this day. And I saw Emma's eyes as those coffee shop patrons hung on my every word. These are the moments we must embrace and remember for what they are: moments of reinforced assurance.

Unfortunately, I didn't get the response for which I'd hoped. My first eight calls were flat nos. A few explained they were in the process of cutting back on outside programs; others were satisfied with current providers. But even these calls gave me lists of prospects. Even if a potential customer is satisfied with a current provider, I knew they'd watch us once we worked with their competitors. If we did what we were capable of doing, they'd want our services.

I heard somewhere that success in cold calling is a numbers game. You do the numbers, you win the prize. The trick is to figure out how many no's you have to get before you can plan on a yes. If it takes twenty no's, and I spend five minutes on each, that means I can plan to get a hot prospect every hundred minutes. Rounded out, that means I can aim at finding my hot numbers at a rate of four a day. Considering the amount of money I would make over the course of a year on any single sale, that was an incredible rate of return. I only needed to sell one prospect every week in order to end up with my 25 corporate clients in six months. If I couldn't do that with eight hot prospects, then I wasn't trying.

Another call. "Mary, I appreciate your time, and I'm sorry to hear things are a bit rough over there right now. I'll call back in six months. I know once you get your head above water, we'll be exactly what you need. Have a great day." I marked it up as another successful step toward a sale. I expressed confidence in her company's potential and my own product as a guide to improve her business.

A couple of hours into the process I stopped to get myself a cup of coffee. I looked down that hallway representing the connecting link to all the pieces in our company puzzle, and I tried to think of ways to strengthen our efforts. From the goals I'd read, every one of them had their own agenda and drive. Each had different expectations they hoped to fulfill by the end of every day.

It was at that moment, while I was considering our differences, that I struck on an idea that might unify our purpose. I waltzed into Otto's office. Not usual for me, and not expected by him. He looked at me first as if I'd lost my mind, and then he settled back with a smile on his face as I explained my vision.

"Otto, imagine with me a moment. Envision a racing team, a pit crew, where everybody is focused in the same direction. Not the entire group of racing teams, just one huddled together around one car and one driver. Those people would have to be led by not just one strong leader, but by an additional leader who shared passionately that same vision. Like the driver and the crew chief working as partners to lead everyone to the winner's circle. The secret to this unifying vision lies in shared goals and similar motivations. Otto, I want this company and everyone in it to share the same unifying vision. I need one other natural leader to jump on board with me, and I believe that might be you. With your shared passion we can get everyone on the same path."

"Now you're talking," he said.

"And a name. We need a name for this project."

"Well, it's military-like. We could simply call it Project Unity."

"That's why you're the man." Still thinking out loud I continued, "The first step is to expose all my agendas and expectations. Every person on our crew must understand the steps ahead of us, and every person must see how aggressive steps forward help meet their own individual goals. Meanwhile, I need to start work on a training manual at some point."

Otto kept smiling.

"I'm sorry," I said. "I need to think on my own, but I'm glad you're on board for this. Thanks for listening."

I decided to go back over everybody's goal sheets that night and identify specific ways our success as a company would meet each person's individual plan. The next step was to become a team more cohesive than any military or sports team. We'd become the driving dynamo that could do anything.

Project Unity. The name had a ring to it. Of course the unifying force would be to develop sales, and every action that wasn't focused on making a sale needed to be trimmed out of the process. This wasn't about making sure our coffee breaks were long enough or that we purchased fancier monitors. It was about focusing on our single objective as a company: to get customers and to service them correctly.

As much as I wanted to stop everything and get sidetracked with a new project, I had to first make sure I was pulling my own 110%. Project

Unity had to begin with Jacob Edwards. I needed to get back to making my sales calls.

By three in the afternoon I'd logged in an impressive number of calls. Several of the prospects sounded promising. I looked out over the park as hordes of people headed to their own destination with their own motives, crossing paths in this tiny blip of nature. A bird perched on a branch waiting for a young boy to drop a bit of the cone his ice cream rested on. A young man on the bench would walk on air if the girl next to him would simply laugh at his worst joke. The hotdog vendor thought of his rent payment coming due while the lady buying a hotdog wondered if she'd be able to look dignified eating a vendor-purchased hotdog in public. A thousand people being driven by their own motives and clear-cut agendas; A thousand people all moving in different directions.

That's why all that energy down there never made a single step in any single, unified direction (as it perhaps shouldn't.) But it would never work to allow my team to pursue their private agenda on company time. Making the company a success was the quickest, most effective way for each to accomplish their own personal agendas.

I began work on a training program for my staff, a weekly meeting that would direct our efforts towards a unified goal. Because I'd made great headway in the phone calls, I took the rest of the afternoon getting ready for the first meeting.

I reviewed all their personal goals and found specific ways to focus them on our overall company objective. Then, I jotted down some of the insight I acquired over the years to help motivate employees. I believed in naming programs and naming manuals. When the moment came to jot something down on the front cover, it was simple. I called this manual "The Glass is Half Full and Frozen Workbook". Opening a text file on my computer, I entered the title. It was definite. I was on my way toward writing a booklet that would change the lives of my employees. Once they grasped the notion of having reached certain goals where they had glasses half full, it would be a revelation to them that they couldn't move forward in life or in business if that half full glass froze in place.

I wrote random notes, as much to myself as to anybody. Besides, I wasn't worried about keeping them in order, or unifying them into themes. All that mattered at this time was that I get my thoughts down on paper. This was the all important brainstorming moment. I could edit them later.

I impulsively put on paper the one thought haunting me all day:

Make sure everyone you work with stays focused on a common goal. Create common goals that can be personalized by every member, making them the medium through which they see themselves reaching their own individual goals.

I thought of another.

Don't run on the people movers at airports. Slow down and savor the moment. Stand still or better yet, walk. Enjoy the exercise. Take a few deep breaths and enjoy the feeling of pressing forward. Being in too much of a rush, ultimately, slows down progress.

They started to pour out, these random instructional thoughts, and I kept writing.

Never surprise your boss. It's his or her job to coordinate the big picture. Being startled by unexpected details will serve no useful purpose in the larger scheme of things. Keep him or her abreast of your progress and aware of possible snags. Letting him or her know where you stand is the easiest way to gain respect and your boss's ever important support.

Always share the bad news along with the good. A strong organization thrives on its ability to deal with obstacles. Having problems buried below the surface is a sure way to create counterproductive time bombs. If everybody has a realistic assessment of both the strengths and weaknesses the company is asked to deal with, they'll all be able to seek a unified, supportive front that can jump over hurdles along the way.

Keep thorough notes. The less you have to commit to memory, the more time you'll have to spend thinking about moving forward. Create filing systems that allow for single entry points and organized data management.

Sometimes naiveté can work in your favor. None of us would tackle most projects if we had a comprehensive assessment of how much work was really involved. Not knowing something can well be the key to pushing forward. If you don't know what you don't know, then you're not aware of what you can't accomplish. The bumblebee doesn't realize (or care) that scientific studies show it can't fly.

Employees would benefit from the value of these insights, and so did I. Knowing these truths and keeping them buried inside, buried even below my conscience, served no useful purpose. Putting them in writing, and posting them as constant reminders, would have a major impact on my personal daily progress.

I needed them and so did my team. We needed to aim toward the same principles. Nothing could be more important to me, as a leader, than developing the character and motivation of my team. I was returning to what took me all the way the first time. The inner wisdom and inner thoughts were surfacing. I wasn't falling prey to the internet craze of get-rich-now, succeed today or bomb.

THE GLASS IS
HALF FULL AND FROZEN

CHAPTER NINE

Thursday, October 13

Checking Account Balance: $338,465

The previous evening we all left on time, enjoyed time with family or friends, and rumor had it Otto and Julie went out for another round of drinks together. This morning, however, we arrived at work facing a stack of empty boxes which had been shipped to our lobby - a reminder that things would be uncomfortable before we soared.

"Busy?" Julie's voice caught me off guard.

"Not yet. What's up?"

She walked in holding an overstuffed 9 x 12 envelope. "The guys in graphics put this package together. They wanted you to look it over and give them the okay to start producing it in bulk."

"I'll let them know later this afternoon. I think I could use your help with something I'm putting together for our next meeting."

I showed her my list and discussed with her the concept of helping employees share the company goals.

"That's the never-ending battle every human resource person fights. I get employees who want to know why they should give one hundred percent when the company never seems to appreciate their efforts, and on the other hand HR people are hounded by bosses demanding employees give more. Far too much energy is wasted trying to appease both sides. If you can create a system where employees see personal benefits while pushing the company agenda forward, you're sure to create one of the most powerful work forces in the industry. You've got my support for anything that tells an employee they aren't just a piece of cheese moved on a whim."

She was right. It was good being validated by a person with experience trying to hold it all together from the middle. I thanked her and promised to look over the promotional package.

How could I explain why unity was so important?

I looked for illustrations from our company's past. Bob came to mind, and the way he wasted money on monitors without permission. But the more I thought about it, I realized that would sound like asking them to side with me against an employee. I stared at the company name on the side of my coffee cup.

I thought about the fancy meeting room and my chic office.

I was guiltier than Bob of spending extravagantly.

Granted, it was my money to spend, plus I had the freedom of authority. But I made my share of foolish mistakes. I made a long and humbling list of all the things I spent money on over the past few months that we could have done without: the office, the cups, plates, chairs, expensive desks, and that $800 painting on the lobby wall. We weren't ready for a $700 oak filing cabinet or the refrigerator in the break room with the ice dispenser and water spout on the outside. David was right. I spent our profits long before they came in. In other words, I bought deep sea fishing gear without a boat. Considering how few of our customers would actually walk into our office, all this stuff could have waited. I didn't know if we'd ever need these kinds of digs. The view was worth it for us, but the décor was too much.

In fact, if I could get back half the money I'd wasted, I probably wouldn't be in the process of moving the business into my basement. It might mean humbling myself in front of my employees, but I couldn't think of anybody that epitomized the problems I saw in our company better than myself.

I empathized with the employees of large corporations who walked out of the offices after layoffs passing through eloquent foyers, and past CEO offices tailored from the executive catalogs.

And then there were the attitudes. I tried to remain in the right circles and completely neglected the workers making it possible for me to get there. I preached that every one of us was expected to pull our share, and I abandoned them, assuming other employees, like Julie, would cover for me. Everything Otto said was true. Moreso, everything Duke said was true. Even Bob had spoken some truth. Someone somewhere once made the point that most bottlenecks happen near the top.

Studies show employees want, more than anything else, appreciation and recognition. They want to know they aren't wasting forty hours a week simply to pay their rent. These needs rate much higher than how much they make and what kind of benefit packages they receive. If I wanted my employees to feel like a team, to give it their all, then I needed to make sure there wasn't one who didn't feel I was personally aware of their efforts and appreciated their hard work.

Napoleon used to have his sergeants provide a list of names of soldiers who had done something noteworthy or had personal life issues. As he rode through the aisles of his 100,000 plus troops, a sergeant gave a hidden signal.

"You're Randolph Olivier, aren't you?" Napoleon asked as the startled soldier bowed his head and whispered, "Yes, sir."

"I heard you dragged Anthony out of battle, ignoring your own wounded leg. We're proud to serve by your side."

Other soldiers might be greeted by Napoleon with

congratulations at having received notice that their wife had given birth. Every one of his 100,000 men was convinced, deep down, that Napoleon knew and cared about him personally. Who wouldn't march days over ice-covered mountains without a break for a leader like that?

I only had twelve people working with me, and with the possible exceptions of Otto, Louise, and Julie, most of them probably wondered if I even knew their names. They were right to be suspicious.

I started a personal diary on every employee charting their progress and listing their strengths. I listed their weaknesses too, so I'd know where to help build them up. I'd make sure I knew all their childrens' birthdays and their anniversaries. Most of all, this wouldn't be fed to me by a behind-the-scenes sergeant: I would make the effort myself.

Along with the diary, I started a journal. I kept notes on what I'd done wrong, what mistakes I made, and the solutions I found. I discovered even though we learn from mistakes, they still hurt. This was a learning phase unparalleled in my life because of the mistakes I'd made. I might have learned, but I also lost much.

I vaguely remembered a birthday cake brought in to celebrate an employee's birthday. I made a point of sneaking around the conference room to avoid getting involved. I missed making an impression and cementing a relationship. With the exception of my core team, I had a building full of people wondering if they wanted to stay with a company about to open shop inside a basement.

I dug into these personal journals, made more calls, reviewed the graphics material, and slipped into a zone.

"Are you going to close up when you leave?" Louise startled me. She stood right in front of my desk. I wondered how long she watched me float around in my own world.

She laughed, "You really were way out there, weren't you?"

"I guess I was."

"It's six, and I'm ready to go home. I wasn't sure if you realized how late it was."

"It's six?" I asked, shocked at how the day had flown by. "No, I didn't realize. If you'll give me a moment to gather my papers, I'll walk you to the parking lot."

"Should I be worried?"

"Why would you be worried?"

"Well, you came in chipper and excited this morning and then locked yourself in your office all day. I noticed you were on the phone until this afternoon, but you just sat alone staring at the wall for much of the day."

I laughed again.

"You should be anything but worried," I said, stuffing things into my bag and sitting on the corner of my desk. "This past week we've had a lot of turning points, but today has been a turning point in my life. Things may not look too good on the ledger books, but we're definitely going to the top. I spent the past three hours thinking of changes that will revolutionize the way we do business. And I think I need to begin by thanking you personally for all the hard work you've been doing even when things didn't look very good."

"You know I'm behind you, Jake."

"I've been far too buried in the day to day business of running this enterprise to stop and thank all of you for the hard work you've done. I know I would never have made it this far, or been ready to pull out of the slump, if it hadn't been for your encouragement and support. That means a lot to me, and ultimately, it means a lot to the company. We're going to make it to the top because people like you make it happen."

"What brought that on?" she asked. "Whatever it was, I'll be glad to buy you another dose."

"Three hours of soul searching."

I tossed the last of my papers in my briefcase and started for the door.

"Hey, you know," she said, "the other night you told Julie to take Otto out of the office and get him a drink? Well, I think they hit it off pretty well."

I looked at her.

"Oh yeah? I thought I saw a new glimmer in Otto's eyes today."

This warmed me, not because I wanted to think about a relationship within the company, but because they both had put in so much work it was great to know they spent an evening together. I'm sure that some of the conversation revolved around the company, but hopefully not all the conversation.

I felt as if I'd finished a weekend seminar on how to motivate and empower employees, and I was dying to try out my newfound skills on someone. I stopped by the coffee shop.

I walked in to that familiar smell of fresh baked brownies, fresh brewed coffee, and found a room full of strangers. I had hoped to see students from the other night, someone readied for deep, meaningful wisdom. Suddenly I wasn't the speaker, the boss, or the wonder-guy. I didn't walk in with implied authority. I was just another guy buying a coffee this time.

The line in front of me was full of people with special coffee needs. Cool autumn weather brings out the best in our coffee sensibility. We want that perfect autumn feel, and it requires a special blend of aroma, taste, and atmosphere. But that's us, the consumer. The young college girl behind the counter was flustered and upset as she ran around adding cinnamon to one, a splash of mint to the other. Somehow she managed to maintain a shallow smile whenever she turned from mixing the lattes and mocachinos. She looked at me, trying to be friendly, as the guy in front walked away sniffing his Kona blend.

"Hi, how can I help you?"

Her nametag said Becky, and her memorized line was anything but genuine.

"You can catch your breath, and then make me whatever coffee you think I'll like." I said, noticing there was nobody else in line. "You can even have a seat if you want until somebody comes up behind me."

"What?" she said, with an edge in her voice.

"You look like they've been running you ragged, and you still managed to get every order right." She smiled and looked down with embarrassment.

I continued, "I'm not in too much of a rush to appreciate hard work when I see it."

"Thanks."

"Make a deal with you," I said reaching for a comment card. "What do you say I tell your boss just how great a job you're doing while you get me a coffee?"

Regardless of how bad her day had been, and little matter what happened after I walked away, this moment she would remember. And it changed her attitude. Perhaps the effects would be more far-reaching than I could know. That didn't matter. What mattered was that at this moment, this young woman felt appreciated.

"How about a double cinnamon mocha supreme?" she asked.

"How about anything that doesn't have cinnamon in it?" I smiled.

"Then how about a Brazilian Misty Mountain Coffee? It's smooth and very popular. And I'd like to toss in one of our onion bagels. I'm allowed two of them a day. I'd be happy to give you one."

"The coffee sounds great. So does the onion bagel, and I appreciate the sentiment, but a very close friend of mine forbids it. He says it gives me bad breath."

"You must have a lot of friends," she said under her breath as she walked towards the coffee maker. Fact was I didn't. I have a wonderful family. I have wonderful employees and colleagues. I have a stranger I feel I have known all my life that talks to me on a bench and who calls me Mr. Frown. But I don't have the kinds of friends this young woman envisioned. Whether business and family takes that luxury away from us, I can't say. But her comment awakened another emotion. A flood of memories of good friends swarmed my mind.

She probably had an entourage of college friends. People she would lose contact with in a few years, maybe stay in touch with a couple on holidays. Friendship wasn't foreign to her. It wasn't foreign to my little Emma or even to my wife. I had always spent my time building businesses. But I could see how my newfound approach to business was sure to make me my share of friends, beginning with the guys down at the office.

I sat at a corner table. The coffee was every bit as smooth as promised. One success of my million-dollar venture was late nights in bars or coffee shops, talking with my equally youthful friends. The world hadn't touched us. We didn't feel societal pressures. We only had goals, which we built in scenes much like this.

A staunch old lady walked up to the counter. The girl behind the counter, perhaps now my friend, greeted her with a warm, caring smile.

"How can I help you, ma'am?"

"You can make me a cappuccino with half a teaspoon of sugar and a sprinkle of nutmeg. But just a sprinkle. Every time I order coffee here someone manages to mess it up."

"I'll be very careful," she answered, smiling as she glanced and winked at me.

"Who are you winking at, young lady? Your boyfriend sitting back there somewhere?" the old grouch asked, turning to find me smiling back at her. I was easily old enough to be the young girl's father, so it was hopefully obvious I wasn't her boyfriend.

"No," the waitress answered as she flipped the cappuccino machine on, "just a good friend."

As I sat in the shop for another hour scratching notes for the meeting, brainstorming as I'd done years ago, I observed the change in the girl. Less than a minute of appreciation made her a cheerful, dedicated worker. She laughed with good-natured customers, and she shared some of her improved attitude with those who weren't. I wondered how much money I would have had to offer that girl to change her attitude so dramatically.

As I walked out of the coffee shop, I glanced at the stars. It was a perfect night. Everything was so perfect, I shouldn't have been surprised that I walked into a sidewalk pothole. As my ankle bent, I reached for the nearest standing item that might catch me, and it was a parking meter. I grabbed it, and it stopped a nasty fall, but a piece of metal sliced across my palm, from pinky to thumb. It was a deep cut. Deep enough that I felt faint.

I sat on the sidewalk to catch my breath. A gentleman came out of the coffee shop.

"Hey buddy, you okay?"

"I think so. Thanks." But we both noticed how badly my hand bled.

"Okay, so maybe not."

"Come on." He lifted me to my feet, forcing me to keep my palm closed. We went to his car.

"I'm a doctor. I'm running you to the clinic down the block. I'll stitch that up for you."

We exchanged pleasantries, he confirmed I was up to date on my Tetanus shot, and he recommended I take painkillers and the next day off. But there was no way. He bandaged me up, sent me home, and I wanted to forget it even happened.

It was almost nine o'clock when I finally got home. I'd called my wife from the doc's office.

Jake and Emma were watching television, a little past Jake's bedtime. My wife smiled as I walked in, and I hugged her with my good hand. After everyone inspected the bandage she said, "The kids want to show you something before they go to bed."

I kissed her and was dragged by Jake through the kitchen and to the door leading to the basement.

"Close your eyes."

I knew they'd spent some time down here sweeping, and earning some pay, but *close your eyes* is rarely a good thing. Once we landed on the last step I was allowed to open my eyes, and there it was. All the bulbs replaced, no cobwebs, no dirt, and the windows spotless. Streetlights shined in enough to work by, so I knew sunlight would make huge improvements. A rug I couldn't allow to remain, because of the effects its color had on my head, was spread across the floor. They had done a stellar job, obviously with the help of Mom.

"Guys, this is terrific. You are an incredible."

"We know you won't keep the pictures," Emma said, "or the rug, or the chairs, or the statue of the penguin in the corner. But we have limited resources."

"You did amazing work. You know I love you guys."

Another nice sleep for everyone. Once work started at the house there would be great obstacles, I knew. Kids wouldn't be allowed in on late nights. I would have to resist the lure of my own home, my refrigerator, the cold six-pack. But for tonight, all was well. It felt like sleeping during a quiet snowfall on Christmas Eve.

I tried to imagine the holiday season this year. Two scenarios played out. The first was a holiday under current conditions where I couldn't afford a pretzel. I replaced that with my new attitude and vision. What the young woman at the counter did for her customers tonight, in a one-minute exchange, I would do for my employees tomorrow. Attitude adjustment. A new company attitude taken into the sales world would change everything. I was learning I'd made a mess of things, and the way to get out of a mess was bit by bit. Nothing happens overnight, and nobody gets it completely right the first time. But we were getting close.

THE GLASS IS
HALF FULL AND FROZEN

CHAPTER TEN

Monday, October 17

Checking Account Balance: $301,136

I woke at 4:30 a.m., 15 minutes before the alarm went off, oddly refreshed. I suppose I woke this early because I hadn't seen Duke in several days. An apple, 30 minutes in my home gym (another present to myself in more fruitful times), and a fresh brisk shower were all I needed. I was ready to tackle the day. It was one of those early Philadelphia mornings visitors see on the cover of postcards. The sun shot beams of light between buildings, frost melted where the sun hit, autumn flowers opened, and nature came to life. I stopped off at an all night coffee shop and got a couple plain bagels and coffee. I'd even changed my attitude on getting Duke his coffee this early. If he didn't mind getting up to help me out, I most certainly didn't mind showing up for some free advice.

"You're early," Duke said, without looking down at his watch as I walked up from behind. I glanced at my watch and noticed I was only five minutes early.

"Good morning," I said with an energy that startled me. I toned down a bit, because I felt like a kid who ate the entire Halloween stash. I was jazzed. "Ready for some breakfast?"

"How'd you manage to get here this early?" Duke asked, not once looking at me. "I always took you for a guy that savored every last minute of sleep he could get."

He was right. I dreaded getting up in the mornings and felt even more threatened by the prospect of walking into the office. Today was different. Visions, goals, and a sense of purpose change things. I didn't mind getting out of bed because I had control over the day.

"I guess I feel good today." I noticed a smile on his face as he studied the antics of a couple of squirrels chasing each other around a tree.

"So, how's your life?" he asked. Even with those glasses on, I could tell he stared me straight in the eyes. It was intimidating, and yet coming from Duke, I knew I needed it.

"My life?" I asked, not sure what he was talking about, which meant I was in for it.

"Yes, your life. How have you been holding together?"

"Well, I've told you about the company and the problems I've had with some of the employees..." I began, but he interrupted me.

"Yes, you've told me about the company and your employees, but I want to know about you. How are you doing?"

"I guess I'm doing okay. I'm doing my share of work and managing to stay out of too much trouble."

He laughed out loud. It was a pleasant sound, but I failed to find any humor in what I had just said.

"Jake, you spent a lot of time in college, tops in college even, and failed to learn the most important lesson of them all."

How did he know I did well in school? I never told him that.

"What lesson was that?" I asked.

"You missed your history lesson. You figured out how to market a product or service, and you learned how to write up a business plan, but you missed the lesson that taught you the importance of what you learned."

"Nobody knows more than I how important that knowledge is," I protested, wondering if this time he had any idea what he was talking about. He hadn't changed my mood, but I was ready to go out and challenge the office. I felt like I was sitting across from an insistent, unsatisfied father.

"That's my point exactly," Duke continued. "You still think all that malarkey you learned in college is important. About the only thing they taught you in college you can still use is how to do math and how to stick to a project until it's finished. The stuff you learned in college was practical for a year or two after you graduated, but with the newer and more powerful computers and unique project-driven software programs, the way we do business changes every day. Anything that worked five years ago is probably obsolete today. It's like trying to keep your records on an eight-track tape."

I took a drink of coffee. I was being schooled.

"The only lesson you need to remember is that success depends on your ability to never stop learning, adapting, evolving. If you have all the answers, you're on your way to failure. Even as we speak, right here at 6:15 in the morning, someone finishes a program or screws the last screw on a piece of equipment that will make everything we depend on obsolete."

I knew this to be true because television equipment had outgrown me. I once scoffed at my parents who let 12:00 AM blink eternally on their VCR and who never used their stereo remote control. But my satellite remote has more on it than I'll ever use. More than I'll ever understand. And this intimidated me. I felt overwhelmed knowing there were things that I didn't know.

Duke continued, "There was a time less than a century ago when nobody kept schedules, especially in this town. Merchants knew sales reps would show up sometime in the next week or two and that was enough. Anybody who dared tell someone they were expected to show up at 9:00 a.m. sharp would have been laughed out of town. Church services on Sunday began when enough regulars arrived. Farm work started as soon as there was enough light to see the plow, and a guy taking a gal on a date would show up sometime in the afternoon and wait on the porch with lemonade and the dog while she got herself ready. Then telephones became commonplace. Suddenly, a salesman could call ahead and make specific plans. Accurate clocks and watches became commonplace. Instead of having to plan for something that might happen a week from now, you could call an hour ahead and announce you were on your way. Can you imagine a salesman trying to do business the old-fashioned way as appealing as it might sound?"

He waited for an answer to a question I assumed was rhetorical.

"I guess it would be a serious problem," I agreed.

"Well, as foolish as that might sound it's not far from some of the nonsense still alive and well in today's marketplace." He paused for what seemed like an eternity; then I broke this weird silence.

"What kind of nonsense are you talking about?" I asked, knowing I was baited.

"Open your briefcase."

I took pride in how neat and organized it looked.

"Show me where you recorded our meeting this morning."

"I didn't write it down," I explained. "I look forward to our meetings. I wouldn't forget about it."

"I didn't ask you if you thought you'd forget about it, I asked you if you recorded it. Jake, I consider it a compliment you feel that deeply about our meetings, but the only way you were going to be able to remember our meetings or anything else happening in your life is to keep those thoughts in the front of your mind. It's like playing music while trying to read. As much as you might think it relaxes you and makes it easier for you to concentrate, it's impossible for you to focus 100% of your attention on reading while you're repeating the lyrics to a popular song. If you had written down our meeting, you could have dedicated more of your memory and more of your day to other events. Who knows what would have occurred to you in that free space? Show me something you did record."

I displayed all the scribbles and notes that reflected a very busy life.

"So where do you fit in time to work on projects and goals that aren't scheduled here?" he asked.

"Oh, I fit them in whenever I find a free moment. That book is just a record of things that have to get done at specific times."

"And how much of the stuff that 'had to get done' last week didn't?" At least half of the entries in the book hadn't taken place. Before I could answer, he reached up and pulled one of the sticky notes I'd pressed against the file flap inside the briefcase.

"What are these?" he asked handing me a note that read, "Call Andrea about the dry cleaning."

"Chores that need to get done. They don't have any specific time limits."

"So, it really doesn't matter if you get your dry cleaning done before your weekend meetings?"

"Well, yes, it needs to get done, but I realize how important it is and…" I interrupted myself, "Okay, I guess I should have put that one in the schedule book."

"No, I don't think that would have been wise. Stop trying to live your life in the last decade." He got up abruptly, again, and started to leave.

"Hold on." I stopped him. "You can't just tell me my life is a mess and then walk away. I agree with you. Maybe I need to get more organized. Can you help?" He slowed but never looked back.

"You don't need me to give you another to-do list. That would make you a slave to something I told you to do, the way you're now a slave to old-fashioned ideas you learned fifteen years ago in college. Work this one out yourself." He kept walking, and I didn't stop him.

I don't know where this guy came from or where he went, but this was the first conversation where I felt I was losing him. I don't know if I was tired of his lecture, or he was tiring of my foolishness. Then I was shamed that I hadn't once used the tools I'd practiced at the coffee shop. I hoped the barista's morning had gone better than mine.

I glanced at my watch, and it was only seven o'clock. The morning joggers made their rounds, and nobody would arrive at the office for another hour. It felt good to have a little time to gather my thoughts before our staff meeting. I pulled out the promo package and looked it over again.

These packets were put together by an incredibly talented and caring team. I had minor comments on font sizes and a couple language usage questions. But this presentation was put together with a tremendous amount of thought, and I was proud to show it off.

It was just after 7:20 when I walked in the office. I heard someone in the conference room, and I wondered if maybe the night cleaning crew was running late.

"Hello?" I opened the door. "Someone in here?" Julie and Louise sat around the table having a cup of coffee. On the table to the side was a full spread of doughnuts, cinnamon rolls, bagels and a fresh pot of coffee.

"Before you run us into your office and tell us we shouldn't waste company money, you should know the two of us bought the goodies out of our own pocket." Julie smiled. "I get the feeling this morning is going to be a turning point, and you can't have a turning point without Dunkin' Donuts and Tastycakes."

I wasn't sure how to answer. I remembered the girl at the coffee shop, and tried to remember when I had ever given either of them a reason to feel I really appreciated what they did.

"You two are too much," I answered sincerely. "I really appreciate this. And I agree, today will be a turning point for our company. But it won't be because of some incredible wisdom I'm going to share. It'll be because people like the two of you who help make this thing work."

"Before I forget, here's that book you lent me," Louise said reaching into her purse and pulling out a worn copy of something I hadn't read since college. This book, part fiction and part non-fiction, told the story of a successful businessman who quit his job to pursue his dream of writing full time. He failed miserably at first, but in the end he succeeded beyond his wildest dreams.

I made a mental note to reread the book. Then I took a moment to write this down as a goal.

"So how did you like it?" I asked Louise as she handed it to me.

"It was incredible," she answered. "So motivational, it makes what we're doing more exciting. It could get bigger than we ever imagined."

"What's the book about?" Julie asked.

"It's about learning how to make your life what you want it to be," Louise explained.

"I often resist that motivational stuff. Kind of empty," Julie replied.

"Well, this is pretty powerful stuff," I explained. "Much of this is about setting goals and watching them get accomplished one by one. Over time, without realizing it, you've set higher goals than you ever thought you'd reach because the small things are out of the way. It doesn't just explain by telling: It shows you how this writer did it."

"Do you mind if I borrow it?" she asked, reaching over to look at it.

"Not at all," I answered making a mental note to buy a second copy. Then, catching myself, I opened my briefcase and made an entry into my schedule.

One of our graphic artists walked in.

"Sandy, how's it going?"

For a moment she stared, surprised I knew her name. I made small talk, as we all did, until she fell into the group. As Sandy told us about her husband and his recent promotion in the National Guard, other employees filed in. I continued to listen to Sandy talk while acknowledging as many of the newcomers as possible.

"Ron, help yourself to some doughnuts," I said. Ron also paused as if he'd forgotten his name. Clearly, I'd hit on something important. If I assumed my employees knew I knew them, I assumed wrong.

Once everybody arrived, I clicked a spoon against the side of my glass and in mock seriousness announced, "Will the first meeting of Winners Anonymous please come to order." Everybody laughed.

"Okay all," I began, trying to make eye contact with as many of them as I could, "I called this meeting to let you know there are going to be some serious changes." As I looked around, I noticed a bit of concern in some of the faces. After Bob's firing, and my last talk with them, that probably sounded like an introduction to the first round of layoffs.

"Yes, even more than moving into my basement. Relax," I continued, "they're all going to be good changes. To begin with, I plan to make serious personal changes. I don't guess it'll come as a surprise to anybody that I have been spending much more money than I should on fancy rooms and chairs like these," I explained, standing to show the chair where I sat.

"I want to begin by apologizing for losing track of our real goal, which is to attract and keep satisfied customers. Once we start doing a good job there, all the rest will fall into place. I have changed my strategy from seducing venture capitalists to gaining and retaining a customer base; anything else is less than we deserve. We're going to chip away everything we do that does not focus on customers."

I continued to explain the importance of making our company goals blend comfortably with their personal goals.

"Every one of you has a long list of habits you've developed over the years. Some of these habits make it possible for you to finish the work you do around here, but many of them keep you from doing the kind of work you'd like. Maybe those methods were great for you in other organizations, but we owe it to our team to evaluate our habits and make a concerted effort to change counterproductive ones. Can anybody give me an example of what I'm talking about?" I assumed I'd get no answers. Again, I assumed wrong. Three hands went up, and I picked Ron from Accounting.

"I still love to write a lot of our figures in an old fashioned multi-column notebook. It's an old habit I got used to long before computers. I guess it wouldn't hurt for me to get better at making my computer do a lot of that stuff."

"You're completely right, Ron," I answered. "There isn't one of us that can't think of ways to use new computer skills. I encourage each of you to figure out ways to streamline what you do by taking full advantage of the computers on your desks."

"I'm always tossed between doing a lot of work and doing a job well," Rick, one of the graphic artists, explained. "I'm forever trying to stay ahead of demand by designing flyers and posters I think we might need someday. I design new graphics for the website, and I like to keep it fresh with custom presentations. I know I'm not always doing my best work, because I'm too busy jumping around to other projects."

"It's important that we place quality above quantity in everything we do," I continued. My responses to these items not on my agenda came from that mystery place within. I jotted notes for our training manual. This was working. As Emma would say, "Quite cool."

"If we're going to rise above the crowd, we must take the time required to do every job the best we can. Trust me. I'm not interested in proving we can pop out a record number of projects. If we do terrible work, we could easily break records. I'm more interested in consistently reflecting the best quality.

"I've taken notes on a book I'm calling *The Glass is Half Full and Frozen Workbook*. It's a training manual for all of us and for new employees. I'll be asking you for input over the next few months. Otto is heading up a similar program called Project Unity, which we'll begin in full force once we get moved. I won't drop all this on you now, but everything we're putting together will involve input from you. Everything with customers in mind, always."

Public speakers talk of connecting with a crowd. It wasn't a 500 person auditorium, but I connected with every person in that room.

We went on to discuss the importance of realistic expectations of our abilities, and how I expected everybody to create realities they would live by rather than pencil in possible events that would never happen.

"Louise, I want to get a copy of that book we discussed earlier for each employee. We're going to make it our goal as a company to think differently. We might start a company book club, in the Oprah tradition, of books we find motivating and uplifting."

The meeting took 90 minutes. We discussed personal goals and interpreted them in ways that made them blend with our overall company goals. If we did well, Ron might be able to build an addition to his house from the bonus we'd give him at the end of next year. Increased productivity using similar techniques would go a long way toward helping Roxanne manage her two kids, school, and work. Louise would be able to schedule and have that dream honeymoon next summer if we could push our company over the top. Otto might be able to date more. Though, I wasn't sure about the matchmaking I'd done.

Otto stood. "Well, if we're all being honest here, I'd like to say I want to develop my skills to someday own my own business. I'm not going to compete with you, boss. I want to work in publishing. But your reputation brought me here, and I swear your success is my success."

"I have no doubt. And that's how business works. You'll reach that goal, Otto. Your work here will train others in years to come, and they will carry on your amazing work ethic.

"My personal goal is to get this company soaring and to spend ample time building up a NASCAR team. You all know I've begun, but I'm eager to delve deeper into that world. But first things first. You all and this company are the priority."

Julie spoke up, "I wouldn't mind joining you on that team, Jake."

"Interesting idea."

We all agreed to make these meetings weekly, and limited to an hour. Instead of spending all day trying to learn everything, I encouraged walking into my office any time to discuss obstacles or to solidify goals.

"On another topic, you should begin packing boxes I've had delivered, as time permits. We'll move sections at a time. Julie has worked up a complete moving plan. Everyone will be there by the end of the week or first of next week. I'll work through the weekend if necessary. You wouldn't believe the place: It's decorated by pros."

I dismissed the meeting.

On the way home that night, I pulled into my favorite coffee shop. A different girl was behind the counter, and I wondered if I could pull my magic on her.

"You guys really do a good job here. Every time I come in here I'm amazed at your work ethic," I said casually as I approached the counter.

"You must be that guy Becky was telling us about. I don't know what you told her, but you really made her day." And this made my day.

Even though it was a Monday, I rushed home calling my sister on the way and asked her to watch the kids. I dined with Shelly at a nice restaurant, not because I deserved it but because she did. I shut the phone off to everything but emergency calls. I spent time with my wife, we had a delicious meal, and we raced home for "dessert."

THE GLASS IS
HALF FULL AND FROZEN

CHAPTER ELEVEN

Tuesday, October 25

Checking Account Balance: $294,117

The next couple days were spent packing for our move. On Thursday we started moving, and I wondered if I'd have time to sneak back over here or even to meet with Duke during the next few days.

Somehow we managed to get everything packed and stacked neatly in the lobby area on the day we'd scheduled. This came at the time when I started receiving interest from customers. The return calls were coming after our packets were delivered. I pulled the trailer used for our race car into the alley, and everybody loaded boxes from the freight elevator into it.

The trailer reminded me that this venture took time away from my NASCAR team. But, business success would lead to success elsewhere. The racing team was growing, and though I wasn't a driver, I was confident in where we headed. My goal was still to have a Cup team in the next five years. For today though, this trailer would house boxes.

We worked like a well-oiled machine with lots of laughter and jokes about leaky pipes. I told Otto he had a penguin sitting in his space, and he laughed as if he thought I was joking.

We each took in one final view from our windows, and I took a picture from my office of the park. I didn't know if I would ever enlarge this photo, or if I'd ever want this view again. From this office, I loved watching the city move in a way I'd never watched it move before. But perhaps I'd learned everything from here I needed. It was time to move on.

By mid-morning the trailer was packed pretty tight, so I suggested we all take a break. We sat on the edge of the loading dock and talked.

"Well, you've either hired the most expensive moving company in town or you've hit rock bottom," I heard a familiar voice echo down the alley and beyond the trailer. A few moments later Duke's familiar ball cap and dark eyeglasses appeared. He was leaning on a new fully-loaded Mercedes Midnight Blue, my favorite color.

"Duke, how are you? That is one hell of a car," I greeted him turning to the rest of the team. "Guys, I want you to meet a man that's made all the difference in the world to me. His name is Duke." I paused as I realized I didn't know his last name.

"How about a walk, Jake?"

I asked the crew to finish their break in another ten minutes and then finish loading the freight elevator for our next run. I hopped off the loading dock and followed Duke down the alley.

"So, it's final then," Duke said motioning with his head at the trailer. "You're really going to move."

"Yes, we're moving, but I really want to continue meeting with you. If you don't mind, I'll be glad to drive over here or anywhere else you'd like. You really don't know how much help you've been." I smiled as I realized how easy this empowering thing was becoming. I hadn't given Duke anything near what I owed him, and it felt nice to compliment him out of sincerity.

"We'll see. I used to own a publishing company called Duke Publishing and was thinking of starting that back up after all this talk with you. So, maybe we'll get too busy for one another."

That sounded pretty definite, so I changed the subject.

"It was a real shame that the Eagles didn't re-sign Tom Alphonso. Without him as a defensive end, I don't know if they can even hope for a decent season."

Duke smiled as he reached impulsively and straightened his cap.

"Really? The season might turn out better than you think."

"Maybe. But, certainly no hope for a Super Bowl run."

"You never know," Duke said with a wink like he'd seen it before.

The late morning sun was just high enough in the sky to reflect brilliantly in his dark glasses.

He slowed his walk and asked, "Have you told your employees that they are nothing more than a commodity?"

I knew better than to react too quickly. Again, completely bewildered, I attempted an answer.

"To begin with, I try not to think of them as employees. I've worked too hard at making them team members, family even, to think of them as anything else. They're very valuable to me, and I would never think of calling any of them a commodity."

"Then I suppose none of them really respects you, do they?" he answered in that authoritatively casual tone that could make lies sound like truth. He could say, "You should wear your socks pink," and I would give it serious consideration.

"How can my treating them disrespectfully make them feel respect *for* me?" I would miss Duke, but not these uncomfortable moments before the lecture.

"How much are you worth to the company?"

I tried to put a price tag on my self worth.

"I don't really know."

"But you know you're the indispensable spark that will make it all work, don't you?"

"Yes."

"Suppose you felt you were little more than dead weight and that your presence, at best, was hurting the overall productivity of the company. How much work would you get done?"

"Very little," I answered thinking of that girl at the coffee shop. As long as she felt everybody suffered because she wasn't pulling her weight, it became a self-fulfilling prophecy. She slowed and did a poor job because she felt she wasn't capable of any better.

"The Eagles didn't lose their defensive end," he said pausing to get all of my attention, "they had to let him go because they decided to offer their running back a $50 million five-year contract extension. The running back may have stayed with them for less, but offering him the extra money made a point. People have a way of living up to our expectations."

He stopped to face me as he always did to drive home the point.

"You like stories?"

"Sure."

"Here's a quickie about a guy in India. Don't ask me where I got this story because I don't remember. The story goes that in India there was a wise man that lived on top of a hill. Word got out that he was coming down to the village to look for a wife. In India, a man is expected to pay a dowry for a wife. An unattractive wife typically costs a man one cow. For two cows a man can get a decent wife. If he's willing to pay four cows, he can plan on any wife he'd like. When he arrived in the village, the wise man looked around at all the women that had come to greet him. Walking past the high society ladies and the beautiful ones, he walked up to one of the homelier women. The woman's father said he'd be honored if the man would accept his daughter as his wife. The wise man asked how much the dowry was. The father laughed and said he'd be delighted to accept a single cow for his daughter. The wise man insisted on paying ten cows.

"Years later one of the village peasants visited the wise man in his mansion. He asked the question everybody in the village asked since the wise man purchased his wife. 'You could have had any woman in the village for four cows and instead you chose to marry a homely one and paid ten cows for her. Why?'

"The villager saw that everything in the mansion was well kept and the garden was beautiful. And then the most beautiful woman the villager had ever seen walked toward them. The wise man explained that as long as everybody told the lady she was at best a one cow woman, she treated herself and everybody around her accordingly. But once he had proven to her that she was worth more than twice as much as any other woman in the village, she started acting like the beautiful, valuable person he saw in her."

"I'm not much into those kinds of parables either," Duke said, "but my point is that every one of your employees offers the company a certain value, and the more they feel you think that value is, the more they will produce. In a business there is no such thing as cost. You never buy anything or pay for anything. Every penny you spend is invested. It needs to show a positive return or it's an unwise investment. Every penny you spend in a salary is an investment you make toward company success. And the more an employee feels you're willing to invest in them, the more they feel they are worth, and the more they're going to produce for you."

We talked for another 20 minutes. It felt good to have someone who knew so much, or who realized so much, guide me through these rough times. I dug for questions I should ask him or policies I needed to get his opinion on. There was one subject that had nagged at me behind everything else going on in our company.

"Duke, do you remember when I fired Bob?" I felt a slight tightening in my stomach. Duke nodded.

"I keep seeing him storm out of my office in anger. I can't help but think there must have been some other way to do that." And then, as if answering myself, I continued, "I hadn't been on top of what was going on in his department. I guess I should have caught the problem long before it became so obvious. I need to set up a system where I do regular evaluations of all the employees six month evaluations."

I paused to think it through for a moment. Duke watched.

"Everyone has written specific goals, and I've asked that they show how these goals align with the focus of the organization. I'll do a review of their performance, and once a year I'll get those who work around them to do a review as well. It would create a great avenue for accountability while providing each individual with a focus point easy to keep in sight."

Duke smiled as he turned to walk back to the trailer.

"I'm sure glad I could help out there. Just be sure you keep a tight diary for each employee, so your reviews will be realistic, personal, and useful. No more exercises in futility."

By the time we arrived back at the trailer, the freight elevator was filled another time, and the warehouse area in front of the loading dock was full of boxes, desks, and filing cabinets. Everybody worked without pause.

"You're doing a good job here," Duke said as we walked up, putting his hand on my shoulder. "Things are going to work out fine."

He'd never done anything like this, but he put his hands out, palms up, and said, "This is where it all happens. Handshakes, hugs, hard work, dancing, and good company: It's all right here."

He closed his hands into fists, and I saw a scar across his hand. On the same hand as mine.

"Be well, Jake."

And with that, he walked away.

By Friday evening, after several trips to my house where we loaded everything into the basement, we'd finished moving. As we pulled up to the building one last time so everybody could get their car, we had an hour to go before the end of the day. I suggested we go to the park.

The meeting felt like a ceremony. I should have held more meetings here. Mother Nature and the Parks Department built a setting I'd paid a ton to look at. I could have used the actual setting for free.

We were in the process of leaving one home and moving into another. As we sat on the grass, we discussed each department and the progress they were making toward our goal of 25 clients in less than six months.

At 5:00 p.m. I thanked everybody, wished them a nice weekend, and told them I'd see everyone at 9:00 a.m. Monday in the new digs. As they got up to leave, I caught a glimpse of a man wearing the familiar purple Phillies cap standing in the shadow of a tree. We made eye contact, Duke nodded and smiled. Then he turned and walked away.

THE GLASS IS
HALF FULL AND FROZEN

CHAPTER TWELVE

Monday, October 31

Checking Account Balance: $251,113

Over the weekend, I spent some time setting up my office. Fortunately, Shelly reminded me of my promise to not take advantage of working at home. So, I stopped working at noon on Saturday, and the whole family went on an unplanned, overnight trip to Baltimore. It was just the outlet I needed to reconnect with my family and to be refreshed for the new journey ahead.

By Monday night our offices were organized and set up. Everyone worked late to clean the last desktop and hang the last photo on the cubicles we'd assembled. I enjoyed the experience of hanging with my family and employees on the same project. I paid the kids $5.00 each, and everyone was happy.

As the last three were preparing to leave on Monday evening, I offered them a chance to come in late Tuesday. "It's been a long hard few days. You guys can sleep in if you like."

"Jake," Otto said first, "I'm ready to dig in. We're saving expenses now and to be quite honest, the view here doesn't do it for me."

"I agree," Julie said, "my newest motivation for working harder than ever is to get out of your basement, boss. No offense."

It was true. Though we'd gone to some great lengths to get more sun filtered in, a little carpeting down, nice lights on the ceiling and on the desks, there was no escaping the fact we were in a basement. I let everyone keep their chairs from the old office. I couldn't part with mine, and I couldn't ask them to do so if I wasn't willing.

"Good. Then we'll be here normal time. I'll promise you this as well; I'll be in the office a half hour to an hour before any of you, since I don't have the commute. I expect I'll be down here later many nights as well."

"Don't sweat it, Jake," Louise said. "This is your home. It's going to be rough since you can't separate the two. Good thing you have an outside entrance to the basement; we would hate to see you in your pajama's!"

Emma walked in with an armload of plates.

"What's this?" I asked.

"Since there are only a few of you still here, Mom fixed dinner for everyone. Jake wants to eat down here; he thinks it will be like a picnic. We'll all join you, but she said to tell you not to get used to it."

Little Jake followed behind with cups. He was dressed in a Spiderman outfit.

"After we eat," he said, "Daddy is taking us trick-or-treating. Let's hurry it up."

"Wow," Julie said, "like father like son."

The Glass Is
Half Full and Frozen

CHAPTER THIRTEEN

Tuesday, November 1

Checking Account Balance: $250,056

Frst thing Tuesday morning we gathered for an informal meeting. The bathroom wasn't running yet down here, so I asked them to keep breaks upstairs coordinated. My family was patient but only to a point. The water cooler would be installed first of next week. Phones should be wired and networked, but it was possible there would be glitches. The final issue was the harsh reality I'd kept to myself, but could now afford to reveal.

"Deal is we're down to six months if everything from this moment forward remains the same. Without the move we were basically finished, but we still have a ticking clock. Six months from today we should consider ourselves without the ability to cut paychecks, pay the phone bills, or run a computer. We'll be out of money.

"That's the bad news. The good news is we have six months to get this company off the ground and build revenue. Because of the sales calls I was able to make just prior to our move, I signed our first customer! I wanted to save the announcement for today. I have three solid leads. Only twenty-four remain to reach our six-month goal."

I sat on the corner of the used oak table we'd set up near the back of the room. I once envisioned a game room in this very spot with a giant plasma television or a small home theater. Never did I think I'd have a board room where my pool table would sit.

"I wonder," Julie said, "if we couldn't share our ideas at this time as well?"

"Absolutely," I answered. Julie gave the most thorough plan of the day, not that I would have doubted it.

"My plan is basic. Starting today, everyone gets involved in the sales and marketing process. All team members able to sell should make a minimum of ten cold calls per week and attend two business meetings a month. I've figured out, through the Chamber of Commerce, how to save a great deal on our health costs. In addition, I've joined a new networking group called NetworkZing★ that meets weekly with business leaders throughout Philadelphia. This group focuses on strategic networking. Since we have no new hires on the horizon, I'm planning to spend my time selling."

"You're comfortable with sales?" I asked.

★ *See www.networkzing.com*

"In another life I sold copiers. In fact, I was the queen of door-to-door copier sales."

Otto spoke up, "I'm tired of looking at this company as a start-up. I'm ready to go the business turnaround route myself. And not only turnaround but jump through a few hoops. I believe with this new strategy of making cold calls and beating the market with our sales pitch, we're going to see great progress. Fast progress."

I jotted down these ideas on our white board and asked people to write down the most meaningful in their notes. Communication within the past weeks had much improved, but it was mostly me to them. I now asked for improved communication all around.

"Once a month we'll meet for a planning session, and there will be planning. I'll expect everyone to report. These gatherings will be during the lunch hour, so bring a bag lunch until the company can justify the cost of pizza.

"I'm putting together a board that will meet on occasion to discuss current marketing strategy and how we can improve. Their job will be on the creative end of things as well searching for new opportunities and areas we might have overlooked. This is Project Unity, and as I mentioned, Otto will head this up."

We planned to trade some of our currently unused equipment with an advertising company for their services. Julie made this contact.

Right now we needed ideas, not machinery, and another team of minds in the advertising industry would do wonders for us.

"The bottom line," I said, "is that for survival it is time to humble ourselves."

"What else?" I asked.

Louise spoke up, "I think we need to watch other organizations for ideas. There have to be untapped areas out there that we can find and learn from. For example, I heard of a machinery corporation that looked at pizza delivery companies to figure how to get product to customers faster. Maybe not thirty minutes or free, but the idea is the same."

"Excellent. As customers come in, let's pay attention to their comments and suggestions. If customers give negative comments, let's find someone who does that area well and figure out how we can do it better. Customers are our main focus now. Every single customer," I repeated for emphasis, "every one of them."

What happened next I didn't expect, but I'd asked if anyone could think of a means of buying us more time. I didn't think the six months would be stretched beyond that time, but after I asked the question, Sally said she'd be happy to give up 10% to 15% of her pay until we got those 25 customers. Otto, after taking on more responsibility, tossed in 10% as well. Almost everyone followed suit. Later that day Julie sent out an email saying that 10% cut from the willing bought us an additional two months. But my hope was that within those first six months we'd have everyone back up to where they started plus bonuses. Maybe then I could even get a paycheck.

My personal cell rang from an undisclosed number. It was Duke, and apparently we weren't done. I was more than relieved. He asked if I could meet him in the evenings now after work. I asked if I could bring my daughter, since we'd started occasional outings to a coffee shop on the way. He said he'd love to meet Emma, but not this time. We still had to discuss things a child would find boring.

After an incredibly productive day, a walk through the park was welcomed. I parked on the far side of Independence Hall to enjoy the stroll. I arrived to the old man, purple hat, giant sunglasses and warm jacket on a relatively mild day. As usual, he was feeding pigeons. I think he kept the Philadelphia pigeon population alive. It was probably ranked by pigeons as the number one city in which to live.

I tiptoed through the flock again, and this time they didn't seem to notice me at all. He'd covered the ground with crumbs and bread.

"Called demand overrunning supply," he said. "Except these consumers don't mind, and the recession in their eating will last only a few minutes. I'll be back in business soon enough."

"How you doing, Duke?"

"I'm the same. I promise. How are things for you?"

"Truthfully, I'm not sure under the circumstances that they could be better. Our team is motivated, all throwing in more than their share of the workload. Many of them even agreed to a 10% pay cut to keep us alive."

"Employees all good then?"

"They feel comfortable telling me if they aren't. Plus, I let them keep the chairs from the old office. We all loved the chairs."

"And your customers?"

"What about them?"

"How do they feel?"

"I guess fine. We haven't done enough with them yet to have feedback."

He turned his head, and again I noticed the scar on his hand. I started to ask, but he was in mid-thought.

"I mean, do they think your product empowers them? Do you understand that if you give your customers a feeling of great power they will be willing to pay most anything? Power is priceless."

"Certainly, I believe our product is empowering. Otherwise, I'm not sure I could believe in it."

"Make sure your customers know this. Even if you assume they know, make sure they know. Current and potential customers. Without giving a little power, your product won't mean much to them."

"Amazing, Duke, how you seem to mention at the right time exactly what I need to hear. I'd considered this but forgot it. You brought it back."

"Well, we're lucky we found each other. That's all."

"You've done so much for me. When do we get to the part where I help you?"

He snickered at first. Then his laughter grew into a full-on, eyes watering laughing session. I wanted to join, but I didn't know what I'd said. Was he implying that I had nothing to offer?

"Jake, look at me. I feed pigeons. In this day and age, I'm pretty invisible to the world. I have a great wife, Jake, and a couple of very grown kids. We keep to ourselves."

"Why haven't you told me? You're almost like a dream, you know?"

"Look at it this way," he turned to me, "if you hadn't met me, you might have ended up here one day, but not driving such a cool car. If you treat your family and employees well, you've repaid me. More than you can know."

"That doesn't make sense."

The birds had cleaned up their abundance of food and were pecking at our feet for more. I wouldn't miss the birds.

"Jake, you see what you've done don't you?"

"Forgot to bring more bread?"

"Sort of. You had a problem, and you could have ignored it."

Two birds, two brave ones, jumped onto the back of the bench and perched right at our shoulders. Duke didn't flinch. I could hear the cooing in my ear. He was holding bread. I was about to make him toss it far away from us.

"You didn't ignore it or you would have eventually gone under: sooner than later. That's a basic foundation of success, but it's huge. You didn't give in; you confronted the problem head on."

He reached into his pocket as my nerves just about pushed me, fleeing, from this bird-infested bench. He tossed a handful of crumbs far into the park. After a barrage of wings and loose feathers, we were free from our avian friends again. He had another handful ready for when they finished up.

"See," he said. "It's just as easy as having a solution and maintaining what works. I wish you luck friend. It's not easy until you figure out what works."

He tossed another handful out to the now satisfied and peaceful pigeons.

"If you don't mind my asking," I said, "what did you do to your hand?"

"When I was younger, I was running to get somewhere and fell in the street. I've learned to walk these days; slow and steady wins."

He stood again, without announcement, and walked away.

"Every action," he said without turning back, "has a result. Every single action, Jake, has a consequence.""

THE GLASS IS
HALF FULL AND FROZEN

CHAPTER FOURTEEN

Friday, November 4

Checking Account Balance: $252,998

T he office buzzed the last day of that first full week. Two major clients signed on. I took Julie to meet with our advertising people and delivered their portion of the unused equipment. We sat together around an oak table incredibly similar to the one we left behind.

"Nice table," I said.

"We just bought it," Charlene, the head ad executive said. "Took a long time, but we decided we'd earned it. We used a jazzed-up version of card tables until this."

"We're familiar with that story," Julie said.

The meeting went forward as I made my vision of a campaign quite clear.

"We want to show potential customers that we're a cutting-edge program, and show established customers how we've empowered them in their endeavors. Furthermore, I want to show how our product changed them. Finally, I want to use real customers, or at least real customer stories, to make it clear."

Discussion never left this topic. Everyone loved the idea, and they talked about various scenarios to make it happen.

As the brainstorming continued, I brought up something close to my heart.

"I'm a big fan of race car driving. In fact, one of my first personal goals when the business begins to grow is to get more involved in my racing team. We only run five to ten races a year now, but within five years we will be at the Cup level. I'd like to start working that into our ad campaign. Both by ads with some race teams I've chosen, and by pulling some of those teams into our team."

The meeting ended with the ad crew excited to get started, themselves interested in our product, and I took Julie to lunch for a meeting well done. As we got out of the car to enter the office she said, "Hey Jake, by the way," she reached into her backseat, "here's the book you loaned me. Amazing. It changed the way I think. It changed the way I work."

"Wanna know a secret that old-timers still teach? The best way to earn respect is to return a borrowed book. It's an amazing act, really. Few people ever ask for a book to be returned, so when one is, it's like giving back a five dollar loan. We expect the thousand dollar loan to be repaid, but never the five dollar loans."

"Always with the advice," she smiled.

Louise waved us over to her desk when we returned.

"Guess who we finally heard from? Andrew Tremmel and the boys. I really think they are all boys because I've yet to hear from a woman in that office. He said he went by our old building and was surprised we hadn't told him we'd moved."

"Yeah," I said, "I guess we should have told him. What else did he say?"

"They like what they hear in terms of customer growth. I didn't tell him we'd moved to your basement, but I get the idea he'd be pleased to know our expenses have bottomed out and our revenue is up. So they want to meet with us."

I hadn't forgotten about Tremmel, but I assumed he'd forgotten about us. I wasn't sure I wanted to be involved with them at this point. It would mean turning over a bit of the company to outsiders. We seemed to be clicking along perfectly now. Their intrusion, especially with Tremmel's arrogance, could stir things up.

"When does he want to talk?"

"When he visited our building he was ready to talk. He wants to know where our hidden lair is, and I suspect he'll be ready to talk when he finds us."

"I'm going to type up a memo by the end of the day. I'd like you to edit it, Louise, and send it to the entire team by morning."

I went back to my office area. Someday I'd have a door. I considered putting my office upstairs to keep myself a little more isolated, but it wouldn't have been fair to the family or the team. I put on the headphones that made it clear I wasn't available should someone need me.

As I let a new idea for the company stir in my head, a way around Tremmel, I typed into Google a search for purple Phillies caps. Nothing came up: nothing on Ebay, nothing on general search engines, nothing anywhere.

But in my search, when I typed in Duke's name (along with some general background information I'd collected), nothing even closely resembling the man came up. Not Duke Publishing, not anything. But the name Duke Jacob did pop up, bringing back a flood of memories of Wharton. As a student I'd written a paper on the history of currency. Jacob Kettler, known as Duke Jacob, ruled Duchy of Courland in the 17th century. Under his rule, their lands reached the greatest prosperity they'd ever known. It could have been a coincidence, but so much about my advisor Duke was a mystery; I began thinking impossible thoughts. In fact, if I hadn't introduced him to the team, and if Emma hadn't seen him sitting with me in the park, I might believe he was just an imaginary friend.

The memo went out, as planned, the next morning. Within an hour everyone replied, not only with overwhelming approval, but many stopped in my office to again thank me for my sincerity to the vision. I proposed in the memo that we thank Tremmel's group for their interest, but we had reconsidered turning over a portion of our ownership to outside interests. Instead, I offered each of the employees stock in the company. Suddenly, not only were the profits part of their motivation, but they were all owners. Every person on the payroll was now part owner.

I politely thanked Andrew Tremmel by phone and told him if he was ever interested in our product to give me a call.

THE GLASS IS
HALF FULL AND FROZEN

CHAPTER FIFTEEN

Tuesday, November 8

Checking Account Balance: $286,135

I didn't hear from Duke again. I didn't need to. I couldn't explain it, but I figured out who he was the morning Julie brought in a box from a client.

"You know, Jake," she said, "when we get to the rehiring stage you might have to hire an HR person first. I'm enjoying selling."

"I don't know that I could trust someone to hire as well as you, but let's cross that river when we reach it. What's the box? Somebody order another two thousand dollar item without permission?"

"Nope, this is from the ad agency. They asked me to give you these."

I opened the box and removed a note.

Mr. Edwards,

This month our company is holding a special promotion on behalf of the Philadelphia Phillies. We've commissioned five thousand commemorative baseball caps for the event. The purple color is to honor our veterans and those brave men and women still in service. The Phillies will wear the purple hats in all spring training games next year. You've never seen these before, but in the future, we hope these hats will remind everyone that life is a team sport, and we are protected by a team of brave souls, so that we might enjoy our lives here in the United States. I remembered you said you like the Phillies, so I thought you would enjoy a hat. I threw in extras for your family.

Best wishes,

Leanna Simons

Inside the box were four purple Phillies caps.

"Thanks Julie."

"You okay? I figured you'd like them, but to bring you to tears..."

"Oh, I love them. Truly. Thanks much."

"If I'd known a hat would move you this much, I'd have bought one months ago. Are you sure you're okay?"

"I am. I, well, I can't explain. But I'm okay."

"You don't look it. You look like you've seen a ghost. Holler if you need anything."

I knew she'd left, but I didn't notice. I was lost in my thoughts.

I can't say I'm a man that believes in many superstitions or even unsolved mysteries. Yet, I want as much as anyone to believe that Frank Capra told a true tale when Clarence the angel made George Bailey realize it was indeed a wonderful life.

I put on that Phillies cap and looked in the mirror. My pulse quickened. I looked at the scar on my hand. I had to sit.

I believed during my time with Duke that the things he said I'd known all along. Things that were intuitive. When I started this new business and let my inhibitions down, I said the opposite of what I'd put into practice. I was scared to do what I'd done the first time around, which was simply to trust myself. I went with the conventions of the day and not the gift for business savvy I'd been given from teachers and my brother, my first business partner who now sailed the world. Duke taught me more than anything to trust in myself, to listen to myself, and to be my own best advisor.

Somehow, without explanation, perhaps through this parallel universe theory I'd read about, I'd met myself, and at the same time I saved myself and my family. That's how I would repay Duke.

***

On the night of the anniversary of the third month after moving into the basement, we'd paid off some of our debt. It was time to have a little party for everyone before the snow started to blanket Philadelphia. This time everyone was invited upstairs. We didn't go extravagant, but I wanted to treat the team to both my family and my home.

Emma worked the crowd like a pro. She'd remembered part of the speech at the coffee shop that night. A few weeks prior I had been invited back to Wharton to speak, and I asked the students what they'd say and what they'd ask if they had the chance to meet their future self. I gave this same mini-speech to the team that night at the party.

"I want to thank you all for being as smart as you are. Because by my hiring you in the first place, it shows that I'm just a little smarter."

They laughed, but there is a truth to that thought. I was surprised at how I'd managed to attract such an amazing crew. And how I knew what part of the crew would have slowed us if they'd remained.

"Because of my role with the company, I've taken a backseat to some of you. Keep this in mind as you go forward, as we all go forward. No matter what situation you're in, the least important is oftentimes the most important. You guys have taken the company in just a few months to a place where I thought it might take a year to reach. I thank you."

What a different scene this was compared to when our story started in that office we couldn't afford. Yet, now we were showing numbers I couldn't have predicted the day we moved into the basement.

"We've made a lot of mistakes," I said, "especially in the

beginning. We learned from those mistakes, I hope, and we won't make them again. We'll make new mistakes without question. Let's all remember what got us here and keep forging ahead.

"And I thank my daughter, my son, and especially my wife, for helping pull us through, helping pull me through. Most of all, I thank a man in a purple Phillies hat."

I put the hat on Jake's head.

"I learned things I'd always known, but I needed permission to take risks again, smart risks. Risks based on a plan of action. Duke gave me permission, and I will never again stop listening to myself. I thank Otto for Project Unity, which gave us that plan of action. We must always do self-checks to make sure we're moving forward in business and in life. We need to keep our glasses half full, and we need to make sure that glass is always flowing and never frozen."

THE GLASS IS
HALF FULL AND FROZEN

Epilogue

After the party that night, Shelly and I tucked the kids into bed. Inquisitive as always, Emma asked, "Dad, what's next?" I patted her on the head, pulled the covers up and kissed her forehead. Shelly looked at me and smiled. She knew the wheels were already turning.

Before retiring for the night, I went down to the office. Looking around at what had been accomplished and reflecting on how I had gotten here, I couldn't help feeling energized. I was surrounded by great people: a motivated staff and a loving family. What's more, I got here by listening to myself.

Taking a little liberty to indulge in my home office, I sat down at my desk and fired up the computer. The training workbook that I had worked on titled "The Glass is Half Full and Frozen" glared up at me. That was it; what I said earlier at the party: "We need to keep our glasses half full, and we need to make sure that glass is always flowing and never frozen." Having found inspiration; I made up my mind. I started typing.

Shelly came down. "Are you coming to bed?"

"I will in a few minutes," I said concentrating on the computer screen. "I have to type some notes while they are in my mind for a new book. I think I will call it "The Glass is Half Full and Flowing."

Watch for Edward DuCoin's next book,

"The Glass is Half Full and Flowing"

in book stores in Fall 2006.

THE GLASS IS
HALF FULL AND FROZEN

About The Author

In 1984, with less than a $200 investment, Edward DuCoin launched Impact Marketing. He quickly grew the tiny company into a thriving organization that was listed as one of the "500 Fastest Growing Companies" for three consecutive years by *INC. Magazine*. Edward built his team to include more than 1,000 members and attained numerous entrepreneurial awards, including a feature in *Success Magazine* that recognized him as one of the "Most Successful Entrepreneurs in the Country" and he is a "Philadelphia Business Hall of Fame Member"

In 1998, Impact collaborated with four other companies and merged into an entity called Compass International Services Corporation which was traded on NASDAQ. Edward served as President of the Teleservices Division and focused on developing an integration strategy for new acquisitions. He was selected to serve as a member of the company's Board of

Directors.

In 1999, The NCO Group, Inc. purchased Compass International at which time Edward returned to his entrepreneurial roots. Since then, Edward has founded three companies, all of which are still operating today. Edward is often invited to speak to business and trade groups on topics such as business operational excellence and marketing.

Edward earned a Degree in Marketing and Entrepreneurial Management from the Wharton School of Business at the University of Pennsylvania. When Edward is not working, he can be found fueling his passion for race car driving. Edward races stock cars nationally. He married his high school sweetheart Michele in 1988 and they have two children, Emily and Edward.

In Loving Memory of

Daniel D'Alesandro

When I look up to the stars I see you
riding your bike across the universe.

THE GLASS IS
HALF FULL AND FROZEN

With Special Thanks

This book would not be possible without the wonderful, talented, patient, and kind people below.

Jason Sitzes provided guidance and magic words as my co-author. Jason, you are a writing guru.

Daniel Yeager is a creative genius whose ideas are reflected on the cover design and graphic design work in all of my companies. Daniel, your ability to make art that works in business is amazing.

Contact Information:

Edward DuCoin
ed@newedventures.com
856-304-2800

Jason Sitzes
jssitzes@aol.com
800-642-2494

Daniel Yeager
daniel@nu-images.com
888-607-1482

Printed in the United States
58265LVS00006B/385-483

9 780977 099900